Nothing to Lose

Nothing to Lose

A GUIDE TO
SANE LIVING IN A
LARGER BODY

CHERI K. ERDMAN, ED.D.

HarperSanFrancisco
An Imprint of HarperCollins*Publishers*

HarperCollins Web Site: http://www.harpercollins.com
HarperCollins®, ♛ ®, and HarperSanFrancisco™ are trademarks of HarperCollins Publishers Inc.

FIRST HARPERCOLLINS PAPERBACK EDITION PUBLISHED IN 1996

Library of Congress Cataloging-in-Publication Data

Erdman, Cheri.
Nothing to lose : a guide to sane living in a larger body / Cheri Erdman.
Includes bibliographical references.
ISBN 0-06-251253-6 (cloth)
ISBN 0-06-251254-4 (pbk.)
1. Overweight women—Mental health. 2. Self-esteem in women. 3. Body image.
4. Obesity—Psychological aspects. 5. Self-acceptance. I. Title.
RC552.025E73   1995
158.1'082—dc20   94–46205

96 97 98 99 00 ❖HAD 10 9 8 7 6 5 4 3 2 1

To the next generation of women,
especially my nieces, Nicole, Erin, and Kristen Erdman.
May you grow up to always accept, respect,
and love the body you already have.

A woman cannot make the culture more aware by saying "Change." But she can change her own attitude about herself, thereby causing devaluing projections to glance off. She does this by taking back her body. By not forsaking the joy of her natural body, by not purchasing the popular illusion that happiness is only bestowed on those of a certain configuration or age, by not waiting or holding back to do anything, and by taking back her real life, and living it full bore, all stops out. This dynamic self-acceptance and self-esteem are what begins to change attitudes in the culture.

CLARISSA PINKOLA ESTÉS
Women Who Run with the Wolves

Contents

Introduction

I am a fat woman. I have carried this identity and stigma since childhood. I cannot remember a time when I was unaware of being fat—even when I was thin.

I am also a doctor, therapist, and educator. At times my professional identity has overshadowed my identity as a fat woman. But most of the time the "fat me" and the "professional me" are merged. Because of this merging, I've had the unique opportunity to study body image issues for women and to understand these issues as only a fat woman can.

While moving toward my own body-size acceptance, I have learned many things. Some of these lessons have come through personal pain—the shame of being fat, the guilt that comes from failing to keep lost weight off, and the assault on my dignity that comes from being judged solely on body size by every stranger I meet.

Some of my learning has come through finding the answers to questions pain has brought to my door, questions such as, Why do I feel shame about my body when I know deep down that I haven't done anything wrong? Why do I feel like a failure at dieting when I know that I have lost at least four hundred pounds in my lifetime? Why can't I keep off the lost weight, since I don't binge or compulsively eat? Why do people continue to judge me as bad, stupid, lazy, and ugly based on my size, when I'm not any of those things?

These thoughts were the seeds that blossomed into a twenty-year odyssey to unravel the dilemma of being a fat woman who doesn't fit the fat stereotype and that continues in the realization that *no* fat woman fits the stereotype. At this point in my life, as I move beyond the fat stereotype, I am experiencing a tremendous freedom and a long-overdue appreciation of my uniqueness as a larger woman. Because I am empowered by these feelings, I have written this book as a way to empower other large women to become free from the shadow of the fat stereotype.

I remember the first time I talked about my body size in the company of other large women (without sharing diets!): It was in 1971 as a part of my women's group. This meeting was monumental to me because it was also the first time I didn't feel guilty about being fat.

Ten years later, in 1981, my mission began in earnest. I developed a workshop that challenged the relationship between eating and body size and questioned the notion that all fat people are compulsive or binge eaters. I was out on a limb since I knew these things to be true only through my personal experience and intuition—and I presented these ideas at a time when I weighed two hundred pounds! It wasn't until much later that I discovered research showing that fat people, on the average, do not eat more than thin people. And it has been only recently that research has challenged the connection between having an eating disorder and being fat (see the notes to this chapter for more information).

In 1982 I taught one of the first college courses to address women and body image, again going against the accepted notion that thinness is necessary to a positive self-image. For the next eight years I explored body image and eating disturbances from an academic and a counseling perspective, which culminated in a doctoral research study on the process of body-size acceptance in healthy fat women. In 1990 I used this research to develop and teach a college course that focuses on building self-esteem in larger women.

Over the years I've talked about this subject, formally and informally, with hundreds of women of all sizes. Some of these women were a part of my study, some have taken my classes, some have been in counseling with me, some are my friends, and some I've met at parties, in swimming pools, and in locker rooms. Women spend an enormous amount of time talking about our bodies!

Now don't get the wrong idea. I didn't start out "fat and happy." My thinking about eating, dieting, and body-size acceptance has evolved over the years as my experience of body size, dieting, and eating behavior has evolved. My first leap of faith was to free myself from dieting in 1987. When I stopped dieting, my eating became more healthful, and my weight stabilized. Then I seriously began the business of coming to terms with living my life in the body I already had—my *larger* body—which is what body-size acceptance is really all about.

Nothing to Lose: A Guide to Sane Living in a Larger Body is based on my personal experience, research, teaching, counseling, and discussions with women, especially larger women. It is my attempt to translate our experiences of body-size acceptance and to share these with you.

Nothing to Lose is written for all women who have struggled with weight and body image, but it is especially written for women of size. Since I am a larger woman, I feel most connected with women who are like me. I know that we have been made to feel guilty by the medical and diet industry and shamed by our well-intentioned families and friends. If you are one of us, I have written this book to help you uncover your uniqueness and to give you hope. My wish for you is that you become size- and self-accepting and that you begin to live the life you want and deserve now.

Nothing to Lose is written also for women of any size who are beginning to realize that they may never reach their "ideal" weight. These are the women who lose and regain the same fifteen pounds year after year and who may not look fat but say they feel fat. If this describes you, then reading this book may help you realize that struggling to attain the "ideal" body may not be worth it—especially if it has become your life's purpose and has been draining your life's energy away from more rewarding pursuits.

For women of all sizes of large, *Nothing to Lose* can offer the information, support, and encouragement needed to move toward body-size acceptance. This will allow you to free up the energy you previously spent on dieting and body dissatisfaction and to use it to do all the things you've dreamed of—to paint, dance, write, go back to school, buy a new wardrobe, move out, change jobs, get into a relationship.

Nothing to Lose is organized in three parts. Part 1, "Myths and Realities," provides information that challenges the many distortions about body size: that thinness has always been desirable, that all fat people are unhealthy and unhappy, and that there is no way out except to continue to try to make ourselves thin.

Part 2, "Who Do We Think We Are?" describes healthy larger women who have become more size- and self-accepting. These chapters deal with our self-concept, our body image, and our spirit.

Part 3, "A Guide to Sane Living," describes the process of size-acceptance that I call the spiral of acceptance. The four phases of this spiral, along with their associated behaviors, are mapped out for you. This section also discusses therapy as an option in moving toward size-acceptance, including how to choose a therapist. (If you are a therapist reading this book, appendix 2 is especially for you. It challenges psychological assumptions you might have regarding your larger clients.)

The concluding chapter is a story written for the purpose of speaking to our deeper selves. It is about a girl-child, Abundia, whose destiny is to learn that her beauty, truth, and purpose in life depend on her ability to value diversity in nature, to listen to her heart, and to accept herself just as she is.

Each chapter of *Nothing to Lose* begins with a story from my life that relates the theme of the chapter to my own process of body-size acceptance. I share these with you because I have learned that telling our stories is one of the most powerful ways to do this work. The chapter theme is expanded upon with research, highlighted by comments from women (whose names have been changed for anonymity) who have talked with me about their experiences of body-size acceptance. Every chapter ends with a list of activities intended to support your effort to become self- and size-accepting.

Keep in mind that this is a process. No one wakes up one day, decides to love her body, and that's it. It takes a day-to-day awareness—from the first look at ourself in the mirror in the morning, to the decision about what and when to eat, to the feel of ourself between the sheets at night. Be patient and gentle with yourself. This stuff takes time. Get support. If you don't want to talk to anyone about this yet, you might want to keep a personal journal. Or find one friend you can talk to about this who will just listen to you (no advice!). Or start a small discussion group with several friends who want to explore these ideas and feelings together. (See appendix 3 for an outline of a support group based on *Nothing to Lose.*) There are many suggestions throughout this book that can help you get the support you need.

I want to say something here about dieting—its relationship to body-size acceptance and its place in *Nothing to Lose.* I believe that a woman of any size cannot come to body-size acceptance while dieting. We diet to change our bodies, not to accept them. By not dieting we are making an effort to accept what is. Because this book is based primarily on a study of nondieting fat women, it does not address at length other problems related to dieting behavior, such as overeating and compulsive eating. I realize that some of you want to learn how to be size accepting yet you need to explore your concerns about your eating and dieting behavior. If you are one of these women, please read appendix 1: "A Word About Dieting and Compulsive Eating" in the back of this book.

Finally, I need to say something about the words *overweight, obese, large,* and *fat.* Our culture has not caught up with the changing attitudes about body weight and size, and we therefore have no judgment-free words available to describe a woman of size. I object to the word *overweight* because it assumes a "right" weight that someone can be over or under. Likewise I object to the word *obese* because the medical community uses it as an indicator of disease.

Throughout this introduction I have alternately used the words *fat* and *large* or *larger.* I realize that you may have felt uncomfortable when I used the word *fat.* This is understandable since this word is used in such a derogatory and shame-inducing way. However, lacking an alternative, I prefer to use the word *fat.* I have learned to become less sensitive to its implied meaning of "bad" and have begun to use it as it is meant to be—an adjective with no moral judgment. Yet I do want you to read this book, so at times I will also use the softer words *large* and *larger.* (By the way, being large also means being powerful, strong, substantial, having weight in the world, having weight to throw around, thinking big, and being bighearted—all pluses!)

At this point you might be telling yourself that you could never accept yourself at this weight. Or you might be thinking that anything (even accepting your size) is better than

xviii / *Nothing to Lose*

living in your world of body-hate. Whatever direction your feelings and thoughts are taking, if you have made the decision to turn the page and continue to read this book, I offer you my encouragement and wholehearted support. After all, when you think about it, you have nothing to lose! So let's begin.

Part One

Myths and Realities

1

Thin Is In—Stout Is Out?

Let's go back forty-some years to 1953. I am five years old and in kindergarten. I am a gifted child with a high IQ. I love school. And I am fat. My teacher, who cares about me, is concerned about my weight. She is fat too, and maybe she wants to save me from a lifetime of shame. Whatever her intentions, she puts in motion an event that changes my young life forever: She convinces my parents to put me in a residential treatment facility for children with "special nutritional needs." In other words, I was sent away from home to be put on a diet. I was there for more than a year. My parents say they visited me once a week on Friday nights, that I lost twenty-five pounds, and that I seemed happy enough.

I don't remember. I have to take their word for it because I recall very little of those thirteen months. In fact I have only one clear memory from that entire year. I was out on the playground with the other kids. It was a bright spring day. Something made me look up from where I was swinging. In the distance, past the fence that separated the playground from the entrance to the camp, was a familiar car. My heart beat faster as I realized that it belonged to my parents. I ran over to the chain-link fence and peered out, hoping to catch a glimpse of my mother. I saw, instead, my brother Patrick. He saw me too. With longing we looked at each other from the prisons that separated us—a fence, a locked car, a camp for special kids, adults who thought they were doing what was best, and a society that was beginning to hate fat people so much that it had devised a place to put fat kids away until they lost weight.

I will never forget what longing feels like, because I was clenched in its hold in what felt like forever as Patrick and I watched each other. I saw it in his four-year-old eyes too. The void of being separated from each other grew larger than ever. The emptiness filled me.

When I look back at that first awareness of having a body, I can still feel a tremendous sadness for the five-year-old fat girl who continues to live in me. I imagine her with all her feelings of being abandoned and rejected in the name of "her own good," and I want to say this to her: Thank you for being brave and strong enough to withstand the separation from your family. Thank you for being resilient enough to bounce back. Thank you for giving me compassion. Thank you for bearing and nurturing the seeds of my future profession. Thank you for being fat, because if you weren't, I wouldn't have the rich life I do today.

As an adult, when I think about this experience I try not to be too hard on my parents or my teacher, who, I'm sure, had good intentions. I've since learned that in 1953 the "war on fat" was beginning, and the world was having second thoughts about fat kids being healthy kids. If I had been born at the turn of the century, my size would have been seen as healthy, as an advantage in fending off any number of childhood diseases.

In fact, reading the history of women's body image was an important part of my own body-size acceptance because it helped reduce my shame for having a larger body. How liberating it was to learn that there were times in our history when having a larger, fleshier body was considered fashionable, healthier, and sexier. If it happened before, it can happen again!

To get you started in this process of size- and self-acceptance, I want to share some of what I have learned. I guarantee that your heart will hold hope as your mind holds the knowledge that the kind of body you have today was once considered healthy *and* desirable.

Before I begin, though, please keep in mind that the information contained in the rest of this chapter is a summary. Since the data I present here will probably challenge much of what you already know and believe about these topics, I encourage you to consult the endnotes for my references and the "Recommended Reading" at the end of *Nothing to Lose.*

A Brief Cultural Weight History

Our culture, like each of us individually, has a weight history. In the beginning, before written history, the ancestors of many of us worshiped an ample, abundant goddess, as evidenced by the Earth Mother of Willendorf, a Paleolithic stone female figure that features a rotund stomach, big hips, and huge breasts. Modern historians interpret her features as symbols of creativity, fertility, nurturance, birth, and bounty. To our forebears, this fleshy ideal of woman represented the importance of the continuation of the human species as seen through the mysterious and abundant female body.

There have been other, more recent eras in which the larger woman was appreciated, admired, and desired. The Greek and Roman ideal of woman was represented by Aphrodite and Venus, both of whom, judging by their depictions in artwork, would be considered fat by today's standards. In the seventeenth century, Rubens and Rembrandt painted women's bodies full and round, reflecting the ideal of the times. When seen through the eyes of a 1990s woman, however, these figures would probably look very fat.

In the late 1800s, the mature woman with a fuller figure was idealized. Lillian Russell, America's sweetheart at that time, weighed over two hundred pounds. The thin woman was besieged with pills, creams, and potions to encourage the ample look. Fashion came to the rescue of our unfortunate thinner sisters by selling them false breasts, thighs, and hips that had natural dimples (which we now call cellulite) designed into them.

During this period doctors also advocated more flesh, because a heavier body was seen as better able to defend itself against disease. For the same reason, the newly formed insurance industry screened out their thinner applicants, preferring the fatter ones.

Thinness, which had been fashionable in the 1700s, became fashionable once again in the 1920s and continued through 1939. The discovery of the calorie (yes, there was a time before the calorie!) and the invention of the penny scale contributed to the thinner ideal by encouraging women to diet and weigh themselves.

By the 1940s, however, fashion magazines were running articles on how *not* to be so thin, and full-bodied pinup and sweater girls became vogue.

The "war on fat" became serious in the 1950s and accelerated in the 1960s with the arrival of the superthin model Twiggy. We have lived ever since in a social climate where fat people, and fat itself, are seen as the evil enemy. The medical, diet, insurance, fitness, and fashion industries have colluded to create this no-fat world.

In all trends (in all of history too) there is a pendulum effect: First we think one way, then we think another. Periods of fashionable fatness have been followed by periods of fashionable thinness. Preferences do change, and society's view of women's bodies today will not be the way society views them tomorrow. These changes can't be predicted. They are often arbitrary, depending on the whims of fashion designers and the inventions of science, and are not necessarily a reflection of scientific "sophistication."

Since history does repeat itself, now is the time to take an active role in swinging the pendulum our way. We can make this happen by changing our minds about our bodies, and by taking our bodies back, making them our personal business and not society's business. *Nothing to Lose,* which contains wisdom from women who have gone through this process, can help you alter your attitudes about your body.

The Infamous Height-Weight Chart

The insurance industry has made its own unique contribution to our current negative thinking about fat people. It created and perpetuated the notion that fat people die earlier than thin people by the publication of the "desirable weight" table. The height-weight chart, which has been tyrannizing us for years, has an interesting history of its own. Knowing how it was developed, and how it has been *challenged,* is information that can empower you in your process of body-size acceptance.

In the 1940s a biologist named Louis Dublin developed the "Ideal Weights" chart for Metropolitan Life Insurance Company based on his statistical research (which is not a scientific causal analysis) of life-insurance policy holders. His research showed a relationship between weight and mortality rates. If we look closely, however, we see several serious flaws in his study.

The people used for the study were not representative of the population as a whole. The people whose weights were represented in the tables were a self-selected group who could afford to buy life insurance policies, which means that for the most part they were white, economically comfortable men, whose northern European ancestry favored tallness and leanness.

There were no standard procedures for collecting weights, and many of the men underreported their weight. Consequently many "overweight" men were categorized as "normal." Furthermore, they reported their weights only once—when they purchased the policy. This meant that no data was gathered on weight fluctuations over the course of a lifetime. We know that people have a natural tendency to gain weight as they get older, yet this information was never factored into the study. Nor did the researchers gather data on what the policyholders weighed when they died, which probably explains why Dublin thought everyone should weigh what was then considered to be the ideal weight for a twenty-five-year-old male.

For example, a twenty-five-year-old male buys a life insurance policy and reports his weight at 160 pounds, although he really weighs 175 pounds. At 160 pounds he is at the "ideal" weight for his age and height. However, he would be considered overweight if his true weight of 175 pounds were recorded. He has an illness at age forty and loses 30 pounds. After he recovers he gains back the 30 pounds, plus 10 more. As he ages he gains another 20 pounds, making him 205 pounds and now 45 pounds over his "ideal" weight.

When he dies at age seventy-two he weighs 195 pounds, but the insurance company still has his weight recorded as 160 pounds, using his self-reported ideal weight as "proof" of his longer lifespan. If his true weight at death were known, he would be considered to be obese by the insurance company's standards, and, according to company statistics, he should not have lived as long as he did.

The most recent insurance study was published in 1983, but it has many of the same problems. The mostly white and overwhelmingly male policyholders reflect only a small portion of the varied and culturally diverse population in the United States. And except for making note of existing health problems, this study does not make any adjustments for those differences that also influence life expectancy, such as smoking and stress.

A number of studies since 1980 have corrected for the flaws in Dublin's research, and they contradict his work. The most important one was done by Ancel Keys. He coordinated sixteen separate long-term projects in seven different countries. *He found that being overweight was not a major risk factor for death or coronary disease in any of the areas of his study!* Numerous other studies done in this country and in Europe show similar results: The worst longevity rates are found only with the *extremes* of thinness and heaviness, leaving a wide range of healthy weights in between. In fact, Dublin's study is the only one that supports his own work!

Dublin also took the liberty to change the meaning of the charts. With the endorsement of the Metropolitan Life Insurance Company, he took the "average" weights in each cell of the height-weight chart and lowered them to "ideal" weights, which everyone was to achieve for optimum health.

He also redefined the meaning of *overweight* and *obese*. Before the 1950s, doctors had always considered obesity to be unhealthful, but they defined obesity as being on the far end of the weight continuum, affecting only a small percentage of the population. Dublin changed the definition of overweight to 10 percent above *ideal* (not average) weight and obesity as 20 to 30 percent above *ideal*. In one move Dublin reclassified average-weight people as overweight, and slightly over-average-weight people as obese—a term that implies an extreme and severe medical condition.

How have women paid for these narrow definitions, these boxes we never fit into, this "proof" our doctors show us of the likelihood of early death if we don't lose those extra pounds? We've paid a very high price in terms of valuable time and money spent on dieting. We've also paid with our self-esteem, which gets lower each time a diet fails us.

In reality these charts have little to do with us because the numbers were gathered from a group of people who did not represent the diversity and genetic makeup of our population as a whole. One recent analysis of the height-weight tables for women showed that a forty-five-year-old woman who was 35 to 45 percent over *average* (not ideal) weight had no loss of life expectancy! The "Ideal Weights" tables show that we are "overweight" merely by someone else's definition of what "overweight" is. And, I ask, how can we be *over* our own weight?

Because researchers have questioned the validity of the height-weight chart as an indicator of health, the "Healthy

Weight" table was developed by the National Research Council in 1989. This table gives "suggested" weights for adults, with the researchers admitting that they have not yet developed more precise ways to describe and measure "healthy" weight. In the meantime, we are left to decide whether our weight is healthy for us by knowing how much of our weight is fat, where fat is located on our body, and whether we have problems such as high blood pressure. This affirms that *we* have to become authorities on our own health as it relates to our weight.

Health Considerations

Let's take a look at the final argument most people (including ourselves) make when confronted with prejudices about fat: "But it's so unhealthy to be fat." This is a belief that is ingrained at an early age. This is a belief about which all kinds of people (including doctors, researchers, housewives, and spiritual gurus) have written volumes. It seems everyone has an opinion about fat and health.

Before we get into the health issue, however, I think it's important to clarify the definition of *overweight* and *obese*. We have seen the insurance industry's arbitrary interpretation of these terms; but how do others go about setting the parameters for overweight and obese? This is not an easy question to answer, because there is no one agreed-upon definition. This is also one of the reasons for the confusion in interpreting the research on weight and health risks. Researchers have attempted to define overweight and obesity by using measures of weight related to height (insurance charts), measures of body fat and regional distribution of fat (healthy weight tables), and weight relative to norms.

Dr. Albert Stunkard, who has researched obesity since the 1950s, has proposed the following simple way of defining obesity relative to norms: mild (20 to 40 percent overweight), moderate (41 to 100 percent overweight), or severe (more than 100 percent overweight). According to his definition, about 35 percent of women in this country are obese; and of this group, 90.5 percent are mildly, 9 percent are moderately, and 0.5 percent are severely obese. Even these definitions of obesity are arbitrary in that they define the condition of obesity by using cut-off points along a normal statistical distribution of body weights (this is not the height-weight chart), without reference to the origins of overweight or to disease.

Stunkard has stated that of the 35 percent of women who are obese (according to his definition), approximately 90 percent are not at increased risk if they do not already have one of the other high-risk conditions, such as high blood pressure, diabetes, or high cholesterol or other body fats. He has also said that since most of the 90 percent do not have these conditions, most of the women who are concerned about their weight from a medical point of view don't need to be!

Compare Stunkard's numbers to the numbers of women who think they are overweight. According to a survey conducted by Dr. Susan Wooley for *Glamour* magazine, 75 percent of the thirty-three thousand women who replied said they were "too fat," including 45 percent who in fact were underweight by the conservative height-weight charts! This means that a lot of us think we're too fat and use the health argument to justify a lifetime of dieting. The truth is most of us aren't that fat (or fat at all), but we allege health concerns to cover the real reason we're uncomfortable with our weight: appearance and society's pressure for us to conform to an image that for most of us is next to impossible to attain.

Definitions of overweight and obesity are not the only arbitrary and misleading elements in the culture's common assumptions about health and weight. Let's look now at some of these beliefs as well as at some facts that encourage us to rethink them. (Check the endnotes and "Recommended Reading" to learn more about the facts that follow.)

Ten Beliefs and Facts Related to Health, Weight, and Dieting

1. *Belief:* Fat is bad. *Fact:* Fat is good for us in many ways, and we need it to live. It's a lightweight, highly efficient form of energy storage. It smooths out the stark irregularities of our skeleton, serving a cosmetic function. It also has a mechanical advantage since it protects our vulnerable joints. It's a good thermal insulator. Fat is necessary for women in menstruation and menopause.

2. *Belief:* Fat people eat more food or take in more calories than thin people. *Fact:* Food intake and fat are not always related. Studies have consistently found no difference in the food intake of fat and lean infants, children, adolescents, and adults.

3. *Belief:* All fat people are compulsive overeaters and

therefore have eating disorders. *Fact:* There is no compelling evidence that being fat results from abnormal eating behavior. Largeness is one variation of human size rather than an indicator of eating problems.

4. *Belief:* All fat people are unhealthy. *Fact:* This is supported by only weak evidence. For instance, some studies show that distribution of fat (pear shaped is better than apple shaped) is more important than the amount of fat in the risk of diabetes and in some cardiovascular diseases. Since most women are pear shaped (carrying fat on hips and buttocks rather than in the stomach area), our risk here is lower.

More important, most studies on the health of fat people have been incorrectly interpreted as cause and effect. For example, it is clear that a small percentage of weight loss can lower blood pressure; but fatness itself does not *cause* high blood pressure. Many large people, myself included, have never had high blood pressure.

Fatness has been shown to have some health benefits as well (see Belief 5). In the United States, fatness has been increasing, yet mortality from cardiovascular disease has been steadily decreasing. In addition, there have been no studies on the health of fat people who have never dieted. This means researchers don't have a clear picture of how dieting affects the health of larger people.

Stress-related illness from living in a fat-phobic country is another unexplored health issue for fat people. Are some unhealthy because of stress from the constant discrimination and persecution they face in this culture rather than from the fat itself? Cross-cultural studies done in societies where no stigma is attached to size and fat (such as Samoa and Guam) indicate that fat people there are quite healthy with no evidence of the "high-risk" diseases that are characteristic of some fat people in North America.

5. *Belief:* Obesity is a disease. (In this example obesity is defined according to my sources, Ernsberger and Haskew, as "elevated body weight relative to a norm or average.") *Fact:* Obesity can be a high-risk *factor* (like high blood pressure and high cholesterol) for some diseases, but it is not in and of itself a disease.

Ernsberger and Haskew also argue that it is no longer appropriate to consider obesity a disease since it has health benefits as well as hazards. Some of the health benefits of obesity include a lower incidence of lung, stomach, and colon cancer and a lower incidence of chronic bronchitis, tuberculosis, mitral valve prolapse, anemia, diabetes type 1, suicide, premature menopause, and osteoporosis. (When was the last time your physician told you that your weight would help build bone mass and offset the undesirable effects of menopause?) Obesity is associated with, *but does not cause,* diabetes type 2, hyperlidemia, hypertension, and rheumatoid arthritis. Finally, any increase in risk from being fat decreases with age, which is the opposite of what would happen if fat were a degenerative disease.

6. *Belief:* Weight is controllable. *Fact:* Weight is largely determined by genetic factors. Fatness has been shown to be inherited biologically (for example, by comparative studies of children and their adoptive versus biological parents). This is especially true of mothers and daughters. The discovery of the obesity gene in 1994 is further proof.

7. *Belief:* Dieting will help you become thinner and is therefore good for you. Dieting can make a fat person thin

forever. *Fact:* Set point theory and subsequent research show that the body has a natural weight, and that all people, fat or thin, adjust their metabolism to maintain that weight. Cycles of weight loss and gain, called yo-yo dieting, affect the body's natural weight by changing the body's metabolism, making lost weight easy to regain despite average or even restrained eating. A phenomenon called diet-induced obesity describes the fate of some fat people who have been on many diets only to regain the lost weight and more. Furthermore, very low-calorie diets can cause damaging physical and psychological side effects, such as gallstones and severe depression.

8. *Belief:* The diet industry, supported by the medical profession, is motivated to find ways to help us lose weight and to improve our health. *Fact:* The diet industry is big business for diet companies, pharmaceutical companies, and doctors and is currently worth over thirty billion dollars a year. The potential fraud of diet programs, with their false and misleading advertising, is under investigation by the Federal Trade Commission, which is finally considering regulating an industry that has never been held accountable by the law.

The most recent trend, which is being supported by some obesity researchers (a few of whom own diet companies) and the pharmaceutical industry (which stands to gain an enormous profit), is a recycled version of the diet pill plan. The 1990s variation includes a redefinition of obesity as a "genetic deficiency" and a "chronic, lifelong disease," so that the prescription now includes taking medication for the rest of one's life. Although these drugs are different from their predecessors in the previous generation, one thing remains the same: No long-term studies have been done on this medication to see what effect it has on the health of larger people.

Since the well-publicized failure of the low-calorie liquid diets (which, by the way, came into existence in the 1980s in much the same way as the new drugs for weight loss are coming into our lives in the 1990s—as a way to "save" fat people from bad health), another weight-loss plan is being promoted—"low-fat eating" (not "dieting," which by now has gotten a bad name). Low-fat eating has been defined by the American Dietetic Association as meaning 30 percent of daily caloric intake from fat and is recommended for everyone's good health. Some low-fat gurus, however, such as Susan Powter, Covert Bailey, and Dean Ornish, are encouraging us to go down to 10 percent. Their idea is that if 30 percent fat intake is good, then 10 percent fat intake must be even better. As an approach to weight loss, however, little research has been done on low-fat dieting, and what research exists shows inconsistent results: Some people lose weight, some don't, and some have even gained weight. There is some speculation that an individual's chemical and genetic composition affects the weight-loss results of low-fat dieting plans.

Low-fat eating is a popular dieting trend among girls and teenage women, yet it has already been shown to adversely affect their menstrual cycles. Having too little fat in the diet also leads to flaky skin, dull hair, and a deficiency in fat-soluble vitamins.

9. *Belief:* Diet and exercise together will make a fat person thin. *Fact:* Good eating and exercising will influence health and fitness more than weight.

10. *Belief:* Fat people are lazy, emotionally unstable, and unhappy. *Fact:* There is little evidence that happiness is di-

rectly related to weight. Researchers have tried to prove that there is a fat personality type but have been unsuccessful because fat and thin people score similarly on most psychological tests. Most forms of psychotherapy for fat people have focused on weight loss. Psychological interventions (of any kind) have been as unsuccessful in helping people with permanent weight loss as commercial diet programs.

Other recent developments support the point of view I am presenting. In 1992 the National Institutes of Health (NIH) changed its position on dieting. Its members reviewed more than a thousand research papers on "voluntary weight loss and control" (dieting) and came to these conclusions: They acknowledged that traditional treatment (diets) are a failure. They said that the public should be warned against participating in commercial diet programs unless these programs are able to produce scientific data on long-term effectiveness (which none has ever done, although some are trying to do so now). Finally they suggest that "a focus on approaches that can produce health benefits independently of weight loss may be the best way to improve the physical and psychological health of Americans seeking to lose weight." These goals are the same as mine in this book!

Listening to Your Own Body's Truth

Almost every week I see media reports that support my nondieting, size-acceptance point of view (along with those that don't). For example, while being bombarded with waif-like models, we are also hearing more stories about girls dying of anorexia because they were trying to emulate this look. While one report insists that eating fat increases our risk of heart disease, another tells us that if we are already free of heart disease, cutting back our saturated fat intake to no more than 10 percent of our daily caloric intake will add only four to thirty days to a woman's life! While "going for the burn" is seen as the premier way to lose fat, another recent study reports that inactive women who were instructed to walk slowly on three-mile jaunts burned more fat than those who walked faster.

Is it any wonder that women are confused about what is true concerning weight, dieting, exercise, and fitness levels related to our health? And while the "experts" are battling it out over definitions of overweight and obesity, whether to diet or not, conflicting reports on health risks and weight, healthy percentages of fat intake, exercise and fitness, who's at risk and who's not, we still have to live our lives!

My position is this: No one knows what is best for me but me. Clearly the jury is still out on the issue of how much weight is too much weight for our body to carry. Furthermore, what has been prescribed by the "authorities" (diets, and go-for-the-burn exercise) doesn't work. This means that *we* have to become authorities on our own body and health.

I learned at an early age not to trust my own experience of my body. This happened when I was sent away from home to lose weight at age five. This experience forever scarred me in my core relationship to my body. At age five I knew at a deep level that my body was my enemy and was not to be trusted at any cost.

It has taken me years to recuperate from that year at fat camp. I'm not even sure I've totally recovered from it. But after thirty-five years of fighting my biology, my hunger, and my culture, I have decided that it is my body, my business. I have done all the right things. I have been on dozens of diets and lost hundreds of pounds. I have been swimming for almost two decades. I have been in psychotherapy. I get regular physical examinations. I eat healthfully. I try to eliminate as much stress as possible from my life. And I am still fat. No one can tell me anymore that my body isn't right. I know that it is.

Your experience in your body, whatever it may be, is your own individual truth. If you are waiting to lose weight before you live your life, don't! You can have the life you want in the body you already have!

As we've seen, our culture's perspective on body size is not set in concrete. In fact, it is filled with potholes. The only truth is your own. It has value for you. You are the expert on your body and on your life. Don't let an arbitrary set of "rules" rule you out of your right to have a life today.

A New Way to View Your Life: Be a Healthy Larger Woman

Here is my basic, and quite simple, body philosophy: Eat healthfully (no diets); move your body because it feels good, not because you think it will help you to lose weight; and get on with your life (regardless of what the scale says). This is not only my philosophy; it is also the outlook of a growing number of other health-care professionals, including nutrition educators, fitness professionals, and therapists. Let's take these points, and my interpretation of them, one by one.

1. Eat healthfully (no diets). By this I do not mean to imply that larger women have unhealthful eating habits. Many of us do eat healthfully. However, some of us are still struggling with chronic dieting, which affects our ability to make good food choices because of the deprivation/binge cycle that dieting sets up. (See appendix 1: "A Word About Dieting and Compulsive Eating" for more information.) To me, healthy eating comprises several factors.

First, learn how to eat without dieting. This is the biggest and often the scariest step to take, because chronic dieters are either on or off a diet—there is no in-between. So when all foods become "legal," there may be a phase of compensating for former eating restrictions, which might include some bingeing, compulsive eating, or overeating. This phase will end, however, if you commit yourself to a nondieting lifestyle. Normalizing your eating takes time, so be patient with yourself if you are trying to break your addiction to dieting.

After learning to eat without dieting, a woman is freer to make food choices that are good for her and her health. Because I do not want to presume to know what your most healthful way to eat is, I would recommend that you contact the American Dietetic Association (ADA) at 312-899-0040 if you need guidelines. The ADA currently endorses cutting back on fats, saturated fat, cholesterol, and salt, and eating more whole grains and fresh fruits and vegetables.

There is another advantage to a nondieting lifestyle: higher self-esteem. One study of 200-plus-pound women found that those who stopped dieting had higher self-esteem than those who still dieted. It's easy to understand why chronic dieters have low self-esteem when faced with the fact that diets fail the dieter 95 percent of the time.

2. Move your body because it feels good, not to lose weight. Exercise has long been used as punishment for being fat, so most larger people have a tendency to avoid exercise at any cost. And if you happen to be a larger woman, it is downright scary to think about going out into the world to walk, bike, or swim—there is always the possibility that someone will make rude comments about your body size.

These things do make it tough to begin, but in my opinion, you must. Why? Because being connected to your body through movement helps to build a positive relationship between you and your body, which in turn helps build your self-esteem. Besides, it feels good to move when you are moving for enjoyment rather than as a way to lose weight. If you're not sure how to start, read *Great Shape: The First Fitness Guide for Large Women* by Pat Lyons and Debby Burgard. These authors are both large women who love to move. Their book will help you choose the kind of movement that's best for you.

Research shows that movement (exercise) will positively affect your fitness level and health more than it will help you to lose weight. So commit to your health rather than to weight loss, and you'll find out just how enjoyable movement is!

3. Get on with your life (regardless of what the scale says). Psychologically it's important to separate your weight and size from your health. Remember that there are unhealthy thin people populating this planet as well as healthy fat people. Focus on developing healthful lifestyle habits, forget about the scale, and begin to have the life you want in the body you already have.

Suggested Activities to Develop an Appreciation of Your Larger Body

PRACTICAL IDEAS

1. Subscribe to *Radiance, the Magazine for Large Women*. Phone number is 510-482-0680. Subscribe to *BBW* (*Big Beautiful Woman*). Phone number is 213-651-0469. Having these magazines delivered to your door can help lift sagging spirits.

2. Become a rebel! Join or support NAAFA, the National Association to Advance Fat Acceptance. Phone number is 916-558-6880. Getting politically and socially involved with other large people can be energizing.

3. Go to the library and check out art books on painters who glorified larger women—Rubens, Rembrandt, Renoir, and Botero. Try to put your 1990 vision of womanhood aside and look at these images to see if you can find why these women are considered beautiful.

4. Find a book about goddesses that includes illustrations or photographs. A good one is *The Once and Future Goddess* by Elinor Gadon (1989) or *Goddesses and Heroines* by

Patricia Monaghan (1981). Try to imagine your link to womanhood and femininity with these earlier images that represent creativity, prosperity, and abundance.

5. Find a copy of the movie *The Famine Within*. It might be available at your local video rental store or your local library. Watch it with a friend and discuss your feelings about it. Write your reflections in your journal.

6. Ask your library to order a copy of the video *Nothing to Lose: Women's Body Image Through Time*. It can be obtained through the College of DuPage, Office of Instructional Design, Twenty-second and Lambert Road, Glen Ellyn, IL 60137. Invite your women friends over to watch and discuss it.

7. Go for a walk. Notice the diversity of nature. Enjoy the walk because it feels good to move your body. Do not time your walk or take your pulse. Just walk until you feel finished. If you find yourself refreshed after your walk, think about doing it again soon—tomorrow or the next day.

8. Live one day this week without dieting. No rules about food. Just listen for your stomach's growl, imagine what you want to eat, then eat it. Move on to your next activity.

JOURNAL ON THE FOLLOWING QUESTIONS

1. Write about your personal weight history. You might want to make a lifeline that includes dates, weights, and significant events in your life. Then put it aside for a few days. Come back to it and reread it. How do you feel about what you are reading? Any insights into your life as signified by your weight gains and losses? Write about these now.

2. Write about the last diet you were on. How did you feel before you made the decision to diet? What significant things were going on in your life when you decided to diet? How long did the diet last? How did you feel when you stopped dieting?

3. Imagine a red light going off in your head every time you tell yourself that you need to lose weight. The red light reminds you to stop and ask yourself another question: What else is going on in my life that I am not paying attention to? Then write about this.

4. Pretend for one day that you are not a larger woman. Pretend that you are your ideal size. Go about your day acting as if you were this smaller person. Write about this experience at the end of the day.

5. Think about the women in your family—your mother, grandmother, aunts, sisters, cousins. What kind of shape do their bodies have? Are any of their bodies shaped like yours? How do they feel about their bodies? How do you feel about their bodies? How do they feel about your body? Write about this now.

6. Imagine how your life might have been different if the insurance charts had never been invented, or if you had been raised in a size-accepting culture, or if you had been allowed to grow just the way your body was meant to grow. Write about your responses to this.

2

Big Fat Lies

I remember standing in line with my professor next to me. My heart was beating furiously. I kept trying to forget that more than a thousand people were in this massive auditorium, focused on the stage. I kept trying to remember that I'd worked hard to get there and that I deserved my moment in the spotlight. I kept thinking about the commencement speaker's words when he said that only 2 percent of the degrees granted are doctorates, and now I was a part of this group. I wondered what would happen as I walked out on that stage when the dean not only read my name but also announced the title of my dissertation study. You see, the title contained the word *fat*, and there I was, a fat woman, about to traverse the stage while the dean said the word *fat*. Now everyone would *know* I was fat! Why did I do this to myself?

My professor, who had been uncomfortable with the word *fat* long before this moment, had asked me earlier to consider another word in the title. "There are no other words," I had said.

Then he told me about this very moment. "Do you want to be standing up there getting your doctor's hood while the dean says the word *fat?*"

"If I can't, then I shouldn't have written this dissertation in the first place!" I responded.

Brave words spoken months before. Now I had to live them out. My knees were shaking. I thought I might faint from the exposure of "coming out" as a fat person in front of all these strangers. I turned to my professor and quietly joked about how I should have listened to his advice. He gave me a reassuring smile and said I would be all right. My turn was next.

Exactly what happened is a blur to me now. I remember my professor putting a hood over me while the dean read the title of my research project. I remember hearing some laughter. I thought, "Are they laughing at me? How could they?" The five-year-old fat girl inside me felt a fleeting moment of shame and vulnerability. Then I heard the applause, and we both felt a bit better. I walked across the stage to shake hands with the president. He said something like, "That's the only dissertation title anyone could understand! Congratulations, Dr. Erdman!" I walked down the stairs and back to my seat. I let out a big breath. It's over. We've lived through this moment—the five-year-old fat girl and the forty-two-year-old woman. And now we have a doctorate!

Later my husband Terry said to me, "You should have seen yourself up there, Cheri. When you walked across the stage, you turned to the audience and smiled your great big smile. And with that smile you destroyed the fat-is-stupid, fat-is-lazy, and fat-is-ugly stereotype."

Who are we, anyway? According to NAAFA (National Association to Advance Fat Acceptance), there are more than thirty million women who wear a size sixteen or larger. That's a large number of large women! We belong to every ethnic and racial group. We are young, old, and middle-aged. We are wealthy, poor, and middle-class. We are married, single, lesbians, and straight. We are lawyers, housewives, teachers, construction workers, child-care workers, and artists. We are everywhere. And if you don't believe it, just spend one day noticing all the large women you encounter. Also notice what these women are doing, and how they are behaving. Probably few fit the fat-is-ugly-lazy-stupid stereotype—a description that is just one of the many big fat lies.

In chapter 1 we learned about society's ever-changing preferences for women's body types. In this chapter we're going to turn our attention to how we can negotiate our larger lives into this thinner era. It's not our fault that we happened to be born into the wrong time! We have to create ways to live large in spite of the cultural, medical, and psychological prison of the fat stereotype.

So what are the fat stereotypes? When someone says the word *fat,* what comes to mind? Picture a fat woman walking down the street. What are your thoughts about her? What do you think people are thinking about you as a fat woman? These are the stereotypes I am referring to—the fat is ugly/ stupid/lazy/emotionally unstable/out of control/unhappy/ unhealthy/unlovable/or (fill in the blank) stereotype.

One way we can defy the stereotypes that follow us like a shadow is to activate our rebellious side. When society says, "You can't!" we say, "Oh yeah? Watch me!" This rebellious attitude positively affects our relationships, our work, our play. The story of my doctoral graduation ceremony is one example from my life. Here are more from other women. These comments address the fat-is-ugly (and therefore nobody will love you) stereotype.

> *Erin:* I had men when I was fat and when I was thinner. So it never really seemed to matter that much. I was 220 pounds when I got married.

> *Lois:* I've never had any trouble getting men. I can go to a bar anytime, and the first person who gets asked to dance is me.

> *Dianna:* Feeling good and being sexual was a part of the process of self-acceptance in my body. Because I've found myself to be desirable regardless of my body size and shape, other people have too.

Others confront the fat-is-lazy and fat-is-stupid stereotype.

> *Dianna:* When I get on a bike, I know that I can ride more miles than most boys can. People don't want to be-

lieve that's true, because they'd rather believe the stereotype.

Grace: The biggest advantage is that people underesti-
mate you. Then you can really come out on top. They
look at you and think you're fat and dumb. No. Sorry.
I'm not.

Marsha: My employers realize that I do a good job. I
think it's an opinion that was built on my actions and my
performance, which has nothing to do with my size,
nothing.

By defying the stereotypes with our rebellious attitudes
and actions, we challenge the culture's views of us with the
reality of our fully lived life. By defying the stereotypes we
learn the most important secret of all: We fat women can do
everything we set out to do and can have everything we want
to have!

We have not always been defiant. At some point in our
life we bought the myth that thinner is better and healthier
and tried to adapt our bodies to the expectations of the
medical industry. Its expectations had become our own. In
the process of doing all the right things—dieting and exercising—we learned that our body would still not conform
and that it would not cooperate with the prescriptions our
doctors had given us. In fact, the more we dieted, the bigger
we got. Even exercise didn't make much of a difference in
losing weight. We thought of our body as our enemy: It
needed to be controlled by even more self-discipline and
willpower.

Society supports the myth of out-of-control bodies. It tries to motivate us to lose weight by feeding us lies (the infamous before-and-after testimonials) about how our life will be transformed when our weight is lost. But many of us *have* lost enormous amounts of weight, and the only thing that changes (temporarily) is our dress size and the *culture*'s opinion of our worth. We also experience a fleeting moment of increased self-esteem—the kind of self-esteem that depends on what the scale says, not on how we truly value ourselves. What have our dieting experiences really been like?

> *Joan:* My mother put me on many diets, trying to make me thin so that I would be happy. None of them really worked. The only time I lost a significant amount of weight was when I went on a six-hundred-calorie diet and lost ten pounds. That allowed me to go on a camping trip that I had wanted to go on, where I gained twelve pounds!

> *Dianna:* I'm fat. I know what that is. I also know that stopping or restricting what I put in my mouth is not going to make the fat go away. The only thing in the past that made the fat go away was hard work and exercise. And even at that, it always comes back.

> *Catherine:* A friend of mine who lives in Minneapolis took off sixty pounds. It cost her two thousand dollars. She put it all back on and more. Two thousand dollars for sixty pounds? Oh, please!

At some point, size-accepting women turn a corner in our thinking: We learn to trust our personal body experience rather than another big fat lie—the medical interpretations of our body experience. One woman I talked to called this the truth about her body. At this point we begin to doubt the medical wisdom about diets and exercise and begin to trust our own body truths.

Sarah: Partially it is the truth of what my body is and what my body says to me when I take the time to listen to it. Part of it is just the truth about my body. I come from a family with largeness in our genes. We are a farming, stocky, strong, muscular people, who use our bodies a lot physically. It's interesting to me that I feel the most attuned with myself when I am doing physical work.

Dianna: I hit a plateau. I could be bicycling fifty to sixty miles a week, but my body got used to that. So I was not burning up as many calories, and I was not losing weight.

Christine: It's been real good for me to be active. I noticed that six months after we started teaching the aerobics class, some of the physical discomforts that I had always associated with being large were actually physical discomforts caused by inactivity and by not being physically conditioned. And I didn't lose any weight, either.

Sarah: If I gave up dieting, my fear was that I would just never stop getting larger and larger. That fear has not come true.

Women have been taught to mistrust our instinctual knowing of our bodies, our body truths, and to trust instead in the external measures of our worth—scales, dress sizes, and mirrored images. The truth is that these numbers, these outside gauges of our importance and self-worth, are more big fat lies.

The scale lies with its numbers, whose meaning is interpreted within a merely cultural context, which we have already seen is arbitrary. In fact, the numbers don't mean anything at all; it's what you're doing about them that has meaning. You can weigh the same 185 pounds (or 115 pounds) and feel bad about the numbers if you aren't dieting and are on your way up or feel good about the numbers if you are dieting and on your way down. One woman I talked to said she has learned to not weigh her self-esteem every morning. This is good advice for all women: Stop weighing yourself! The scale lies.

Dress sizes lie too. Ask anyone in retail clothing and they'll tell you that dress sizes change with designer, manufacturers, styles, and times. There never used to be a size one, but of course there have always been women that small. A size fourteen from the 1940s and one from today are not sized the same. Women's bodies have always come in varying sizes and shapes, but clothes haven't. So it doesn't make sense to take pride in oneself if one wears a size five yet hate oneself if one wears a size twenty. Advice I've heard from women in the clothing industry is to buy clothes for fit, comfort, and style. Remove the size tag from your garment if the number bothers you, because the size lies. It has nothing to do with your value in the world.

The mirror is also a liar. What we see in the mirror is rarely what others see when they look at us. Our mirrored image reflects what we perceive about our body and our behavior around our body, and not how it actually looks. In fact, how others see us is an individual perception based on *their* judgments about body size. It's all in the perception, not in the reality.

Here's an example of how the mirror lies. We go on a diet, have one "good day," and "feel thinner." We look in the mirror and we *see* ourself thinner, which is actually caused by the perception that we have done something "good" to change our body. The next day we eat a pint of ice cream and thereby create a "bad day" and a perception of "being bad," which the mirror reflects as a "fat" body. Our body has actually not changed at all, but our perception of it has, based on whether we have been "good" or "bad" around food.

I'm not suggesting that you never look in a mirror again. I am suggesting, however, that you be aware of your feelings about your body and eating behavior and integrate this into your perception of your mirrored reflection. Because the mirror, like scales and dress sizes, lies to us, it is important to be gentle with your reflection.

Our body truth does not lie. It has shown us that diets don't work. Because of this some of us have stopped dieting. Others of us, however, still believe something is wrong with us or we wouldn't be fat. We then trade in the diet doctor for the head doctor, attributing our weight to emotional causes. Some of us have been in therapy for reasons other than our weight and have had our therapists insist on making our weight the issue. So what can we do when we face the psychological interpretations of our body? How can we handle the consistent misinterpretation of our psyche by our well-meaning, friendly psychotherapists?

Since the psychology of fat has been determined by the culture and not by fat people themselves, here we find more big fat lies. The women I've talked to have already accomplished an enormous feat by defying society's stereotypes about fat people and by trusting their own body wisdom rather than the medical interpretation of their body type. These attitudes and actions also affect their psychological processes in that these women have removed the stigma from being fat. This means that the way they live in itself challenges the notion that being fat always means being psychologically unhealthy. It transforms the notion that fat is "bad" into an understanding that human beings simply vary in size. Having this attitude reduces the stress they feel about their body size and frees them to pursue other important life goals.

The women I've interviewed have had various opinions about therapy as an asset in their process of body-size acceptance: Some thought it helped, but most did not. As a therapist, I was surprised by this. But then I remembered that my own earlier experiences in therapy (before I was a therapist myself) were not always positive when it came to my body size. Considering this, I would recommend therapy only if you can find an enlightened therapist who is not fat-phobic. Please read chapter 7, "If You're Considering Therapy . . . ," for a lengthier discussion of this topic.

So where are the big fat lies? One lie lives in the culture, which views fat as something bad. We have found *our truth* by defying society's stereotype of what a fat person is and by becoming ourself instead. Another lie lives in the health industry, which tells us that diets work for everybody and that all fat people are unhealthy. We have found *our truth* by listening to our own body wisdom, which tells us how to take care of our health without dieting. Another lie lives in the psychology of fat, which tells us that unresolved emotional problems contribute to our body size. We have found *our truth* by removing the stigma from being fat and by thinking of our body as one variation in human size and beauty. We've seen how scales, sizes, and mirrors lie to us too.

The biggest fat lie of all, however, is that *we* have a weight problem. The truth is this: *We* don't have a weight problem. *Society* does.

Suggested Activities to Develop Your Own Truths for Challenging the Big Fat Lies

PRACTICAL IDEAS

1. Throw away your scale. If that seems too radical, then put your scale away and stop weighing yourself. If that seems impossible, then put your scale away and take it out once a month to weigh yourself. If that's too scary, then put your scale away and take it out once a week to weigh yourself. If that still sends waves of anxiety through you, then put your scale away and take it out once a day to weigh yourself. Get the idea? *Throw away your scale and stop weighing yourself!* If these ideas don't help, figure out your own way to break your addiction to weighing yourself (and your self-esteem). Trust yourself. Your body knows how much you need to weigh. Remember, the scale lies.

2. The next time you go to your doctor's office, tell the nurse, "I'd prefer not to be weighed today." If she makes it into a big deal, tell her you'll talk to your doctor about it. When you talk to your doctor, tell her that you both know that you're a larger woman, so you feel that weighing yourself every visit isn't necessary. If they insist, you can still refuse. Or you can get on the scale with your eyes closed and ask them not to say your weight aloud. This action is important especially if you've broken the weighing-in addiction at home.

3. Go through your closet and take out anything that doesn't fit. Give it to someone who is the right size for it, donate it to a woman's shelter, or take it to your local resale shop. Now take out the clothes that fit. Look at the size. How does this number affect the way you feel about yourself? If you notice your critical voice being activated, stop! Get scissors, cut out the size label, and try to remember how you feel in this piece of clothing—comfortable? stylish? beautiful? If you don't feel good in this garment, then put it in the cast-off bag with the other clothes. If it feels comfortable, stylish, and beautiful, put it back in the closet and forget about your size.

4. Make a list of all the things you are not doing until you lose weight. Everything. Then go through the list and order the items by their level of risk: The activity that would be the least risky for you to do at your current weight goes at the top of the list, and the riskiest item goes at the bottom. Now head for the least risky item, take a deep breath, and do it! Notice what happens in the world. Does it end? Do you get laughed at? Does it feel good? Make it a habit to do the next thing on your list as soon as possible. As you grow in your

confidence, make it a habit to add other things to your list. You'll soon learn you can have the life you want in the body you already have.

5. In what way can you defy a stereotype about being a larger person? Ask for a bigger chair without shame? Go swimming at the local pool? Own more than one bathing suit? Tell someone that you no longer believe that dieting is in your best interest? Eat whatever you want in public? Ask yourself if you are willing to do this act of defiance today. If the answer is yes, then go out and do it.

6. Find some enjoyable way to move your body. This can be any way you want. It can include the obvious things, such as taking a walk, or the not-so-obvious things, such as gardening or taking a yoga class. If one thing doesn't keep you interested after you do it, try another. Or try alternating the kinds of things you do to keep your interest up and your body moving. The important thing is to find your body's truth about movement.

7. Try to pay attention to your body's hunger for one day. Try to eat what you really want to eat, no matter what it is or when it is. The important thing is to find your body's truth about your hunger.

8. Subscribe to the newsletter *On a Positive Note,* written by Carol Johnson, founder of the "Largely Positive" support group in Milwaukee, Wisconsin. It usually contains a summary of the most current research about obesity, along with helpful hints about living large. Address is P.O. Box 17223, Glendale, WI 53217. Cost is about twelve dollars a year.

9. Purchase a copy of the video *Bodytrust: Undieting Your Way to Health and Happiness.* This video includes helpful information and interviews with women who have gone

through a nondieting, size-accepting process. It can be ordered through Dayle Hayes, R.D., 2110 Overland Ave., Suite 120, Billings, MT 59102 (800-321-9499). Cost is about thirty dollars.

10. Purchase a copy of the video *Yoga for Round Bodies* if you are interested in this form of stretching, movement, and relaxation. Contact Plus Productions, Box 265, Scotland, CT 06264 (800-793-0666).

JOURNAL ON THE FOLLOWING QUESTIONS

1. What are some of your own stereotypes concerning fat people?

2. What are some of the ways in which you have already defied the stereotypes about being a larger woman?

3. What are some new ways in which you are willing to defy the stereotypes about being a larger woman? Imagine yourself doing them. What does that feel like? Write about this now.

4. Ask yourself if you are willing to do an act of defiance today. If the answer is no, then write about why you aren't willing to do this now.

5. What do your body truths mean to you? Have you ever felt connected to your body's wisdom? When? What was going on?

6. Think about how many diets you've been on this year. Ask yourself how much money you've spent on dieting over the past twelve months. Write that number down. Now think about the past five years and how much money you've spent on dieting. Write that number down. Now try to stretch this

idea out over your entire lifetime, and write down your estimation of how much money you've spent over all the years you've been dieting. Look at these numbers. What are you thinking? How are you feeling? Write about this now.

7. Notice other large women you encounter today. Notice how they behave. Notice how they look. How do they help to reduce the stigma that all fat people carry? How does your behavior and appearance help to reduce this stigma for other large women?

8. If you've ever been in therapy, try to remember your therapist's attitude about your body. Did you feel safe and comfortable there? Did you go there thinking you had an emotional problem related to your weight? What did you learn about yourself?

Part Two

Who Do We Think We Are?

3

From the Inside Out: Self-Concept

It's difficult to pick just one moment from my life that captures the essence of the way my self-concept developed. Let me instead try to illuminate the process by presenting a dialogue between my adult self and my child self, who is affectionately known to me as "Cherry Pie."

> *Me:* I'm trying to understand who I am today in relationship to who I was growing up as a fat girl. Can you help me find my beginnings, the roots of my self-concept? I have a feeling that you hold the key.
>
> *Cherry Pie:* Every kid devises some way or another to make it to adulthood alive. Your therapist self calls it a coping mechanism, but I like to call it my coping tricks. Like the five-year-old fat girl

on that TV talk show who called herself "fluffy" instead of "fat." That's real creative thinking! I had lots of tricks that got us through grade school and high school. Then in college another part of you took over—the rebellious and wild part. But her story is for another time.

Me: Yeah, I remember her real well. It's *you* that I'm having a tough time getting back to. Was it that long ago? Or is it just too painful to remember?

Cherry Pie: It's both. But I remember. I'll never forget what I had to do to get through childhood and adolescence while everyone was picking on me about my weight.

Me: Like what?

Cherry Pie: Like having a rich inner life. Remember how much I liked to read? All those Nancy Drew books, *Anne of Green Gables, Little Women,* and the others. When things got tough, I escaped by reading about how other girls lived. And remember how I used to keep a scrapbook with a collection of every piece of paper that had any meaning to me at all? I kept those so that I would have a visible reminder of my worth when people started picking on me for being fat.

Me: That's right. I used to spend hours reading and putting together those scrapbooks. Were those your only tricks?

Cherry Pie: Heavens, no! My favorite trick was to ignore the whole fat-girl trap by pretending that I wasn't fat. I would have "fat memory lapses," acting as if I were a normal *little* girl. I mean, I knew I was fat—how could I totally ignore it when everybody reminded me of it every chance they got? But I also knew I was other things, like smart and creative. Remember when I won a prize in third grade for writing that poem about spring? And a certificate in fourth grade for my drawings? And the blue ribbon in Campfire Girls for my embroidering? And recognition for my writing in an eighth-grade competition? Remember wearing a chartreuse tutu in a tap dance recital in second grade? I do. It was the most beautiful costume in the whole world. Do you think that I spent one moment up there thinking about how fat I was?

Me: I had really forgotten about those things. By bringing them up, you're reminding me of others: spending second grade in a special school for gifted kids and learning French while I was there. Those were really big things!

Cherry Pie: Yes, and the key you asked for is this: *Being fat, although central to everyone else's view of me, is not central to my own view of me.* I mean, I knew I was fat, because everyone kept reminding me. And I was hurt that everyone saw the smart and creative parts of me as secondary to the

> fat me. I feel like they never saw *me* at all. But I
> saw me, and that's all that really matters. And
> because of it, you are who you are today.

What does "self-concept" mean? In this era of self-help books and support groups, this expression, along with *self-perception* and *self-esteem,* is commonly used, often without a clear sense of its meaning. Before getting into the heart of this chapter, therefore, I need to explain how I am using these terms. I'll begin with self-perception, because it is the building block of the others. Self-perception is the ability to understand and be aware of oneself. Self-perception means that we presume to know our attitudes, traits, and motives from observing our behavior. Self-perception is the basis of self-concept.

Self-concept, loosely defined, means how we think of ourselves. For instance, I think of myself as a woman, a teacher, a daughter, a wife, and a homeowner, among others. They are a reflection of some part of myself, a role I play, a relationship I have.

When I add an evaluation to these functions, I am working on defining my self-esteem—building it up or dragging it down. If I say I am an attractive woman, a good teacher, a loyal daughter, a faithful wife, and a smart homeowner, I have made movement toward building up my self-esteem with positive assessments. By contrast, if I say I am an ugly woman, a terrible teacher, a disloyal daughter, an unfaithful wife, or an uninformed homeowner, I am obviously lowering my self-esteem with my negative judgments.

It's important to understand these three terms because they help us form the basis of knowing ourself from the inside out. In other words, what we observe, think, and feel about ourself from the inside forms the basis of our outward behavior. Cherry Pie told me that the key to my self-concept was my early self-perception that to me being fat was always secondary to being smart and creative. Having that self-perception built a strong self-concept early on and allowed me to act out my idea of myself regardless of anyone's idea of me. Being fat, and being judged as flawed because of it, wore down my self-esteem at times. But it never did me in completely, because deep down I knew there was more to me than being fat. I clung to that self-perception like a drowning person clings to a life preserver. It has saved my real self from dying.

As I grew older I acquired more experiences to affirm this basic self-perception and to strengthen my self-concept. However, there were many times when others' negative evaluation of my body became my own. I had to work hard at countering these messages in order to raise my feelings of self-worth. So have the other larger women who have talked to me about their struggles with body image and self-esteem.

Those of us who have given up dieting and have learned to accept our body size seem to share a common thread in our self-concept. This commonality is that we lead an "inner-determining" lifestyle. This term simply means that we nondieting large women are always in the process of deciding about ourselves and our lives from the inner self. This deciding does not happen just once in our lives ("I'm large and I'm OK about it." The end.). We keep making the decision to listen to our inner voice and its wise message of self-care and self-love. This allows the truth of our inner voice to grow in strength and clarity until it drowns out the other voices (usually negative) that are competing for our attention.

The opposite of inner-determined is externally determined. This happens when an individual's worth is decided by someone or something outside herself without her direction or involvement. For instance, when it comes to body size and shape, the culture has already decided what is acceptable for a female before she is even born. We've had practically no voice in making the rules about the acceptability of our own bodies. And this cultural determination affects our lives every day.

All the women I interviewed for my research were leading an inner-determining lifestyle, constantly deciding what was right and true for them from their own inner voice.

Catherine: I figure that if something is wrong, part of my body will let me know.

Joy: One of the things that helps me a lot is focusing more on my body and the way it feels rather than on the way it looks.

Grace: I guess I don't have to please others anymore. I have to please me first. I don't think I'll lose weight to impress anyone anymore.

Michelle: I know by whatever standards there are in the world that I'm pretty. But sometimes I feel like I wouldn't be acceptable to somebody else, and that makes me feel sad, because more and more I'm finding myself acceptable to me.

Catherine: If you have to live for someone else's approval, get a grip.

Dianna: My therapist has helped me to stay in touch with who I am and to be centered in myself. That has been important—almost like little jewels with which I decorate the inside of me. These jewels create a wonderful brilliance, and this has really enlightened me to take my life one step farther.

How can you become more inner-determining? From the collective experience of the women who have shared their stories with me, I have learned that there seem to be several pillars that support an inner-determining lifestyle. These pillars are knowledge, introspection, assertion, independence, and open-mindedness.

The cornerstone of being an inner-determining woman of size is having an adequate knowledge of our health, dieting, and body-image issues. We obtain this knowledge through listening to our own body truths first; we then verify them with the historical and medical perspective that supports our experience. It is very important that you become familiar with this research, because it makes confrontations much easier to handle. When you stop dieting and start accepting yourself, someone (including your own critical voice) will inevitably challenge your behavior. The last argument is always, "But it's so *unhealthy* to be fat." When that moment comes, you will feel much better about yourself if you know a research study or two that says this isn't always the case. Armed with this information, you can stick up for yourself. This builds on your self-concept because now you can add "knowledgeable" to the list of ways you know yourself to be when it comes to understanding the relationship between your larger body and your health. This will help raise your self-esteem, because it is good for you to know these things, and it is good for you to stick up for yourself. It allows you to lower the volume on the negative voices inside your head.

> *Christine:* I think the first occurrence that opened the door to self-acceptance for me was the recognition of how horrible the dieting statistics are, of how few people succeed in taking weight off and keeping it off. That really raised the possibility that I was not going to ever lose weight permanently.

> *Dianna:* Learning as much as I could about nutrition and theories of body weight and size really helped.

> *Joy:* I think one of the things that has helped is learning. I think I have accepted my weight, my body, everything because I have learned so much about it.

While becoming knowledgeable about these things, we also need to reflect upon them. Introspection is the second pillar of an inner-determining lifestyle because it allows us to consider our experiences as fat women and to come to our own conclusions about our bodies and health. Introspection allows us to compare what they say about our body with what we experience and know about our own body truths.

> *Erin:* Underneath all the overweight stuff is who I am. I do know who I am, and it's not a fat person with no other identity. There really is more to life than whether you're overweight or not or whether you're on a diet or not. When I actually started to pull these ideas apart and examine them, I became more accepting.

> *Dianna:* I'm not separate from my body. This is me. Without this body, I'm not me. My body has been a weight that has anchored me to the earth in painful ways up until my self-acceptance.

Combining knowledge about fat and dieting with introspection about who we are as women of size often strengthens our stand when we are confronted by others about our size. Becoming assertive about our personal body issues is the third pillar supporting us as we become inner-determining. As I mentioned earlier, when we stick up for ourself, we feel good about ourself.

> *Grace:* My doctor does not bother me about it, and if he did, I would go somewhere else. I'm the same way with him that I am with anybody else: "My body, my business."

> *Joan:* In years past I would have listened to a doctor's whole lecture about weight, but today I don't even bother. I say, "Listen, if you want to give me a cream for

this skin rash, then fine, write out the prescription. If you don't want to, if you're determined to put me on a diet that I have already told you I am not interested in, then fine—I'll walk out of here, and you don't get paid for this office call because you did not do your job. I mean, I came in here because of this skin rash. I don't need your diet. I don't want it, and I'm not buying it."

Joy: I was very excited about my family coming. We weren't even five minutes into the visit when they started: "You should lose some weight." I said, "You came over here to have a good time with me. Now you're talking about my weight. I don't need this."

Anne: When I was pregnant, it was impossible to find maternity clothes for anyone over a size eighteen. I would go into maternity shops and say, "This is ridiculous. Don't you think there are women over a size eighteen who get pregnant?"

Along with assertion comes a sense of being independent, which is the fourth pillar of leading an inner-determining life. Being independent means deciding for ourself what we want and then acting on it, regardless of other people's opinion. Sometimes the women I talked to would refer to this independent quality in themselves as rebelliousness.

Dianna: I was the black sheep. I was smart and got branded early on for being intelligent but without any common sense. I rebelled more.

Sarah: There's a piece about embracing my largeness that makes me feel like I am counterculture. This gives me permission to actualize myself and to be all these other parts of me that don't always fit together.

The final pillar of an inner-determining lifestyle is being open-minded. We fat people are often discriminated against because of our bodies. This puts us in society's out group, on the edge, off in left field. We know what it feels like to be chosen last, if at all. It is therefore natural for us to have empathy for others who, like us, are watching from the sidelines. Developing an open-mindedness about others who are also discriminated against gives us empathy and support for our own position in society. We're not bad; we're just different.

Sarah: Feminism really set me up for accepting diversity and refusing ordinary, rigid boundaries. I look back on that now and am pleased at having opened myself to a lot of other people's choices to be who they are.

Michelle: If you really care about somebody, you are going to have to accept them however they are.

Abby: The "yes" part of being fat is that it has given me a sensitivity to other people.

Leading an inner-determining lifestyle is an important part of building our self-concept and raising our self-esteem. But it is not the only piece. There are other ways to get out of a fat mentality and into our life. These pieces include living in the present moment, having fat-positive perceptions, and feeling our competence, confidence, and power as women of size.

Ever hear the saying "Be here now"? This was the title of a popular book in the 1970s and a slogan for a whole generation of people turned on to Eastern philosophy. It means that the only moment we have is this moment, so be in it and live it with full awareness. This is a difficult thing to do, especially in our goal-oriented society. It requires discipline and constant reminders to stop looking back and to quit looking forward. What does this have to do with building a size-accepting self-concept? Everything!

Women who have eating and body-image concerns tend to live in the future of "when I lose weight" or in the past of "when I was thinner." In its most extreme form, the effort to become thinner becomes central, and all other activities are put off until the weight is lost. The plan does include resuming these activities when the perfect body arrives. But for many that day never comes.

The nondieting, size-accepting women with whom I've discussed this issue share a self-perception that encourages them to stop living for the day they lose weight. Since they no longer have an interest in dieting, they have turned their attention to their other life goals. They have a sense of getting on with things, of choosing to stay in the present reality of being larger and making the most of it. After years of putting off living until they lose weight, they derive deep satisfaction from having a life in the body they already have.

Christine: At one point I made a list of what I would do if I were thin and resolved to do some of those things right now. I had three things on the list: buy a new wardrobe, get my pilot's license, and become more active in sports. I wound up doing all those things.

Joan: Dieting puts your whole life on hold. I don't know how many years I have on earth. I would just as soon live them than sit around and diet through them.

Catherine: It's taken a long time. I think, "By God, if at the age of forty-four I haven't figured this out, I am going to be miserable for the rest of my life." And I don't have time to be miserable.

Christine: As long as your whole life is lived with an emphasis on losing weight, you end up without a life.

Sarah: We're all going to die. What matters is how we live the life we have right now.

From a psychological view, living in the present moment is often used as an indicator of the creative and self-actualized person. Carl Rogers, the founding father of humanistic psychology, talked about "being in the now" as a way for the self and personality to emerge from the experience of living rather than the other way around. Women who have chosen to stop dieting and get on with things keep accumulating evidence that they can have the life they want in the body they already have. Fat or thin, life goes on, and we can choose to live it fully in the present.

This builds a self-concept that includes an awareness that you are able to do something meaningful with your time. For instance, Christine's self-concept now includes being a pilot and an athlete. This kind of addition to our self-concept improves our self-esteem because we have a better chance at success with the other things in our life that don't revolve around the failure of dieting. How do you think Christine feels about being a pilot and an athlete? Great! You too can feel great about your successes.

Another piece to the size-esteem puzzle is the building of fat-positive perceptions. When I first suggest this idea to my groups and classes, they are initially perplexed. What could be positive about their size? Larger women have spent most of their lives hating their bodies so much that we can't see past the hate to the largesse that's hovering close by.

The larger women I've talked to over the years often mention that in the process of becoming more size- and self-accepting, they begin to notice ways that being fat serves them in their lives. They begin to view being fat as a positive quality, in either a literal or metaphorical sense.

Dianna: To me fat meant that I was noticed, and I was a presence that people had to contend with. So when I was able to identify those positive aspects of being fat, I was able to reclaim them as parts of my personality and not something that was simply a facet of my physical appearance.

Sarah: I know that I am not meant to be a small person size-wise. I also know that I'm not meant to be a small person in my gifts. I think of myself as being large no matter what size I am physically.

Joan: When I'm dressed well, I can enter a room and make a statement: "Here's a sharp fat lady, and she looks good." I think I have more presence.

Dianna: I don't want to lose weight. If I lose weight, fine, but I'm always going to be a weighty person, a substantive person.

Being large can mean being powerful, strong, substantial, having weight in the world, having weight to throw around, thinking big, being bighearted, and so on. In fact, think about how many terms the culture has to elevate the idea of big and large—except when it comes to women's bodies! But some of us have begun to see that our size makes a statement about us that is positive. The statement "I am a big woman" is part of our self-concept. Beyond that statement it's possible to think, "I am a big, powerful, beautiful woman." This kind of thinking makes major inroads to improving our self-esteem.

The final piece of the size-esteem puzzle is allowing ourselves to feel our competence, confidence, and our power as larger women. Nondieting, size-accepting women have time and energy to achieve goals other than losing weight. We constantly read about fat women who hate themselves, who feel like failures in the world, who buy the message that they have to lose weight before they can have a life. Well, there's more to our story than that.

Allowing ourselves to recognize our competence in the world is the first step. Women who are focused on dieting and weight loss often put other achievements somewhere at the end of their list of who they are. These successes take second place to the when-I-lose-weight fantasy. When you decide to put dieting and weight loss at the bottom of your list, however, you can begin to acknowledge the other things you're good at. You can begin to know yourself as a competent woman even if you don't have the perfect body. Perfect bodies don't come with a guarantee that we'll also be competent in them.

Anne: I get a lot of affirmation in what I do professionally. I have gifts. I speak really well, and I have the ability at times to move an audience. To me, being able to touch someone and have them either weep or laugh with you is a powerful gift.

Abby: This change is also bringing a creative aspect out in me. It's been wonderful.

Dianna: I remember thinking at the end of writing my thesis, "If I can do this, I can do anything. I can take myself seriously as an intellectual."

Erin: I can help people who have been in incredible pain all their life to feel better, so it must not be a big deal that I'm overweight.

Michelle: I'm competent, responsible, and loyal. I'm all those things and more.

Confidence is the natural next step. After all, it's courageous to take an "I'm good!" attitude when you're a larger woman. This courage often spills over as confidence in the rest of our life. Having confidence builds more confidence.

Joy: As far as body size and weight are concerned, I feel fabulous. I feel fabulous when I walk into a room. I went to a wedding once and wore this purple outfit—purple from head to toe. We were late. I said to my husband, "Just think of the grand entrance we'll make." I mean, people are going to notice me anyway when I walk into a room, so I might as well do it with style and feel good about it. When we walked in, they were playing, "Hot, Hot, Hot," and I said to my husband, "See, they're even playing my song!"

Catherine: Yeah, I'm fat, and yeah, I'm really terrific!

Michelle: There is something in me, as I've grown stronger, more secure, more confident. People don't insult me about my size. I used to get that all the time.

The result of being aware of ourselves as competent, and showing the world how confident we can be, is feeling empowered, regardless of weight. Not all size-accepting larger women feel this kind of power—the kind that comes with their size. It is a special place of being completely in touch with your largeness—in body and gifts—so that you know that your power in the world is enhanced through your size.

Dianna: Trusting my body is such an empowering thing because it means that I not only accept myself, but I see myself as more powerful in the world because of my size.

So what kind of self-concept does the nondieting and size-accepting woman have? How does she show herself to the world from the inside out? As Cherry Pie's words wisely reminded me, being fat was never central to my view of myself, regardless of what anyone else thought. My basic self-concept sustained other parts of me too, which allowed me to create and thrive even under adverse conditions.

The women whose words I've shared with you in this chapter teach us other important lessons. Things such as learning how to live an inner-determining lifestyle in which you make decisions according to your own inner wisdom. Things such as getting smart about the medical and historical evidence that supports your basic right to be healthy and happy in the body you already have. Things such as learning to become reflective about your body experience rather than taking in the culture's interpretation of your body. These women encourage us to become more assertive in and about our larger body, to be independent in our views and actions in the world, to become open-minded and empathic toward those who are discriminated against for being different.

If we learn from self-accepting women, we will also try to live for today, to develop a positive view of what our fat does for us in the world. We will become aware of our competence in the world as if it were money in the bank. We will wear our confidence as if it were a three-carat diamond ring. We will feel the power that can come from being a woman of size and substance, an abundant woman, a woman who is worth her weight in gold!

Suggested Activities to Build Your Self-Concept and Raise Your Self-Esteem

PRACTICAL IDEAS

1. Read the medical information that supports your body truths. Use chapter 1 as a primer, but read more. See the endnotes and "Recommended Reading."

2. Begin to keep a journal in which you can reflect on what you are learning as you do your research compared with what you are learning by listening to your own body. Begin to know your body truths this way.

3. When someone makes a positive comment to you about your appearance, practice saying thank you.

4. When someone makes a positive comment about something that you are doing well, just smile and say, "Thank you."

5. If someone says something negative about your body, such as "Have you gained weight?" or, worse, "You've gotten really fat. Why don't you go on a diet?" just answer with, "My body, my business," and walk away.

6. Try to think of other ways you can stick up for yourself if someone starts picking on you about your size. Write them down. Practice saying them out loud, to yourself and to a size-friendly friend. Have your ammunition ready. Imagine that someone is picking on you. Imagine that you are saying something to stick up for yourself. That's being assertive!

7. For more ideas on how to assert yourself regarding your body and size, purchase a copy of the videotape *Nothing to Lose* by the Fat Lip Reader's Theatre. Address is c/o Wolfe

Video, P.O. Box 64, New Almaden, CA 95042. Skits done with humor and style. Highly recommended.

8. Take an assertiveness training class at your local community college. Practice these skills in relationship to your size.

9. Think about the ways in which you see yourself as different from the crowd. When was the last time you behaved that way? Remind yourself to do something today that builds your sense of yourself as an independent person. When you see the opportunity to be independent, act on it.

10. Think about another out group—an ethnic minority, the homeless, battered women, the aging—and see if you can find a way to reach out in thought or action to embrace them as connected to you.

11. Make a list of all the things you are putting off doing until you get the perfect body. Begin to do them. Begin collecting your evidence that you can have the life you want in the body you already have.

12. Think about the ways in which being a larger woman has been beneficial to you. If this seems too contradictory to what you have been thinking about yourself, ask a size-friendly friend to tell you how she sees your large size as an asset. Have this thought in your mind: "Being larger has some benefits for me." Wait to see what kinds of ideas come to you.

13. Make a list of ways in which you are competent. These things do not have to be earth-shattering or indicators of fame or anything grandiose. Perhaps you're organized or can create a comfortable and pleasant home. You may have a sense of style in your clothing or may make the best

lasagna in the neighborhood. Think about the things you do every day that you rarely pay attention to and begin noticing them. Think about the challenges you've faced and lived up to (even if nobody else knew about them). Think about your big and small successes every day. Keep this as an ongoing list by your bed or in your journal. Read it often. Add to it often. Build your knowledge of yourself as a woman who has other parts to herself in addition to being large. These parts of yourself show that you are competent.

14. Make one positive statement about yourself (from your list) and say it aloud to someone. If this seems too scary, say these things aloud to yourself first, just to get used to hearing them come from you. Then practice saying them to a trusted friend. Soon you'll be able to say them to lots of people at appropriate times (in a job interview, for instance) without feeling embarrassed about being good!

JOURNAL ON THE FOLLOWING QUESTIONS

1. What are the various parts of yourself? List them. Write about them so that you get to know these parts of yourself better. What are their good qualities? How do they get you in trouble? What do these parts need from you? Want from you? See Ferrucci's book, *What We May Be: Techniques for Psychological and Spiritual Growth Through Psychosynthesis* (1982) for more ideas about working with the parts of yourself.

2. Make a list of the roles you play and other things you notice about yourself. For instance, a woman, a city dweller, a consultant, a daughter, a cat lover. These are parts of your

self-concept. What do you think about your self-concept? Write about these things.

3. Now go through your list and evaluate these things. For instance, a smart woman, a culturally satisfied city dweller, a busy and productive consultant, a loving daughter, an affectionate cat lover. Try to emphasize the positive aspects of these parts of yourself. This will help you raise your self-esteem. Write about what you know of your self-esteem. How do you feel about your self-esteem?

4. Think of the ways in which you are already living an inner-determining lifestyle. Think of the ways in which you are not. How do you feel about this?

5. Reflect on your assertiveness. When are you assertive? When is it hard for you to stand up for your rights? With whom is it easy to be assertive? With whom is it hard?

6. Write about your ideal life, your ultimate fantasy of living on planet Earth. Set it down with all the rich detail you can imagine. What would it be like to get up in the morning? What would you spend your time doing? Where would you be living? How would you spend your money? Who would be around you, if anyone? Go ahead. Give yourself permission to imagine it and to write all about it. Now pick out some ways in which you can begin to make your real life look like your fantasy life *without changing your body*. How does this feel to you?

7. Write a letter to yourself in which you pretend that you are writing to your best friend. She has a serious illness, and you have this one last chance to say everything about her that you have always wanted her to know—all the ways in which she has been important to you, all of the kind things

she has done for you, the wonderful qualities she has, the ways she has affected your life and that of others. Say everything. Put the letter away for a week. Bring it out and read it when you have a quiet moment. Really let yourself feel what it's like to be the person this letter is about. Take it in. When you're done reading and feeling this letter, write about this experience in your journal.

4

From the Outside In:
Body Image

During the 1993 Thanksgiving holiday I had a profound body-image experience. My husband, Terry, and I were spending the night with my brother. After dinner I asked my brother if we could watch a home video of our grandmother, Nan. Since her death seven years before, I had avoided watching any of these videos because I felt it would be too painful. That night I was ready to have the magic of video bring her back to life there in his family room. I didn't realize that the tape's magic would bring back another visitor from the past and put her too into the family room with us.

My brother randomly reached into his bin and came up with a tape from Thanksgiving and Christmas 1983—exactly ten years before. I saw a lot of things on that home video that moved mountains of emotion within me—Nan as if she had never left us, two smiling aunts who are gone now too, younger versions of my parents, brothers, nieces, and me—weighing 135 pounds.

I was shocked to see my image on the TV screen. I watched myself with disbelief. Who *is* that woman? She's skinny. She has no breasts. She's acting weird.

I didn't recognize me in her at all. I felt embarrassed and ashamed of myself sitting in my brother's family room in my 235-pound body. I felt myself tighten up as I waited to hear comments from him and my husband. Comments about how much better I looked back then.

The first one to say something was Terry. When we were married in 1990, I weighed over 200 pounds. And he wasn't around in 1983. I held my breath a little as I heard his voice begin. "Is that you, Cheri? You aren't acting like you." I breathed a little easier because he didn't say anything about my body. Then he said, "You're really skinny. I don't think I like you that skinny." I let my breath out. He hadn't criticized my 1993 body by praising the 1983 one. He wasn't going to demand that I go on a diet immediately. He wasn't going to ask me for a divorce because now he knew that I once was thin. At that moment I deeply understood the reason I married him: He loves me exactly as I am.

Then my brother said something about how different I looked—younger, different hair. He didn't make any comments about my weight, but I felt his judgment that I looked better then, when I was thin. He thinks everybody looks better when they're thin. That's his opinion. And he's entitled to it. After all, he's male and lives in this culture too. Even though he knows my pain and my political position on this topic, he doesn't deny that he'd rather see my body weighing less than it does.

But my brother wasn't the only one judging the before-and-after image of my body; I was too. My first reaction to seeing myself thinner was, of course, to see myself as more attractive then. I was becoming more and more uncomfortable as I sat there and watched the thinner me on TV.

While I watched, my mind also went back to those exact moments in 1983 as if I were living them in the present. It was Christmas Day, and I had just returned from a week's vacation in Mexico. I flashed back and suddenly remembered how fat I'd felt on that trip. How agonized I was at putting on a bathing suit. How unattractive and unsexy I felt. How embarrassed I was when someone I met on the trip commented on my heavy thighs. How uncomfortable I was around food, since I was still trying to diet. Oh, my God! I remember. I thought I was fat. I felt fat. But I wasn't fat. I weighed 135 pounds. I was thin.

My mind kept working while I watched. I was smoking cigarettes then. I was in an unhealthy relationship then. I was eating and dieting compulsively then. I was feeling depressed then. I was acting like, well, an impostor of myself. Whoever was on that screen wasn't healthy, and surely she wasn't me. I kept reflecting that since then I'd stopped smoking. I was in a healthy marriage. I'd stopped dieting and had consequently stopped eating compulsively. I'd been through therapy and considered myself to be relatively sane. I'd finished my doctorate. And I'd gained weight.

In reflecting on that experience in my brother's family room, a question occurred to me: If I took a snapshot of me in 1983 and one of me now and asked people who didn't know me, "Who is healthier and happier?" what kind of response would I get? I bet everyone would say I was healthier and happier in 1983 weighing 135 pounds. But I know the truth. I wasn't.

———————

Having bodies is the primary way we exist in the human world. Our bodies are our companions in life. Our bodies bring us our pleasure and our pain. We can choose to deny our bodies and live primarily through our intellectual or spiritual nature. However, our bodies always remind us of their importance by demanding our attention to their needs to breathe, eat, drink, and sleep.

Our judgments about having a certain type of body—thin, fat, or in-between—come from the values of our culture. And as we saw in chapter 1, these judgments change with the times.

I like to think that having a functioning and healthy body is the best type of body to have. Yet fashion, economics, actuaries, and men's preferences usually determine what is acceptable for women's bodies. Being healthy is not enough. We must be thin, fit, and muscular, which are now synonymous with being healthy. We must also have large breasts on the stick-thin body, making the ideal woman resemble a well-developed adolescent boy. Most women can't conform to this standard. So most women, even thin women, learn to dislike their bodies. And almost all women learn from an early age to fear getting fat.

Body image is a term we hear often these days. What's it about? I like Marcia Hutchinson's idea of body image from her book *Transforming Body Image: Learning to Love the Body You Have.* Simply put, body image is the way we experience our body on a visual, kinesthetic, and auditory level. Our visual experience refers to how we see our body in the mirror or in our mind's eye. Our kinesthetic experience refers to how we sense and feel in our body. Our auditory experience refers to how we think and talk to ourself about our body. I like to add what I consider to be another important dimension: The visual, auditory, and kinesthetic experiences of our body image are affected by our culture's attitudes toward certain types of bodies for women. Given the capriciousness of cultural tastes in desirable body types, it is no wonder that most of us feel a little (or a lot) crazed about our bodies and our body image.

What role does body image play in a woman's life today? In 1986 a body-image survey of thirty thousand men and women was conducted for *Psychology Today*. This survey's results were compared with a similar survey the magazine had done in 1972. Considering overall appearance satisfaction, the 1985 survey found that 38 percent of the women were generally dissatisfied with their looks—a higher percentage than was reported in 1972. Fifty-five percent of the women reported weight dissatisfaction, especially in their lower and mid-torsos. Even more women, 63 percent, were afraid of becoming fat. Compared to men, underweight women were more likely to consider themselves normal, and normal-weight women were more likely to consider themselves overweight. These results support the notion that women hold rather extreme standards for an acceptable body.

Other results of this study showed that while most "overweight" women disliked their appearance, many of them also felt good about themselves. Women at their ideal weight, however, reported being constantly preoccupied with their supposedly fat body parts. The researchers concluded that having an ideal body does not guarantee happiness, nor does having a less-than-ideal body guarantee a life of unhappiness.

More women are becoming aware of the differences between the body image the culture pushes on us and the reality of living in a woman's body. Books and articles have appeared that encourage women to accept themselves as they are. However, the change-your-body-into-a-thinner-one message lives right alongside the accept-your-body-as-it-is message, and this creates confusion. What is more, some books market themselves as accept-your-body-as-it-is but are really diet books in disguise.

In a recent *Chicago Tribune* "Womenews" section, for instance, an article about how to cultivate a healthy body image was placed next to an advertisement for liposuction and cosmetic surgery, complete with a photo of a very thin and almost bare-breasted woman looking seductively from the page. Likewise *Vogue* recently published an article confronting the cult of low-fat dieting—this between the pictures of stick-thin models. And Lane Bryant, a merchandiser that has been selling larger women's clothes for decades, uses size eight women as models in its catalogs. No wonder our feelings about our body change so drastically from one moment to the next.

So how do we begin to change our mind to fit our body instead of trying to change our body to fit our mind? A big task, but not impossible. Let's begin by taking a look at the experiences of women who have shared their stories with me and at my interpretations of these stories.

Even though the women I talked to are living large in a culture that devalues their size, they are still able to come to terms with their body image in creative ways. When I began these interviews, I believed that a woman needed to have a realistic body image to have a healthy sense of herself. This belief came from my counselor training. What I heard from these women, however, was very different. Some of them were talking about seeing themselves as smaller than they actually were. And they knew it. They admitted to underestimating their body-image size. I had expected that a fat woman who accepted her body size would also see herself as she was: fat.

I began to let go of my counseling theories because I soon realized that larger women who have this reduced body image *are* psychologically healthy. Underestimation of size can be a healthy response for larger women because it assists us in moving toward a more complete acceptance of ourselves—and a life more fully lived. For us, a smaller body image allows us to act as if we were "normal" size. This "acting as if" allows us to move through life unencumbered by the burden of fat stereotypes. We can see ourself as smaller and act as if our size were not an issue for us or anyone else.

When counselors work with anorexic or bulimic women, one goal is to help them develop a realistic body image. This is necessary because their distorted self-image, which accuses them of being too fat, compels them to either binge and purge or starve to death. Developing a realistic body image is in the service of these women's survival. The larger women who took part in my interviews, by contrast, did not have the eating disorders of anorexia or bulimia. For them, having a smaller body image was really a tool for sound living. Because this is positive, I call it the creative body image. We are re-creating our body image in order to minimize the effects of the fat stereotype in our life.

I have my own creative body image. When I get ready to swim every morning, do you think I remind myself that I am putting on a size twenty-two bathing suit? No. If I did, I would probably not put it on. In fact, I probably wouldn't even own a bathing suit. Which means I would never go to a pool, and I would never swim a mile a day. I'd be at home worrying about how fat I was and wishing I could lose weight so that I could go swimming!

Other large women who talked to me had stories about their creative body image too—they just didn't call it that.

Erin: It just didn't make sense that I could weigh 270 pounds and go work out four to five times a week. So I feel like I have an inner body that is very athletic and fit, and then there is this other body that I really didn't feel was mine until I saw a picture of it.

Patricia: There is this myth that says that if I'm a large size, I can't do anything. So therefore I can't do anything unless I adjust my image of myself.

Abby: I think that I am a thin person. I feel like I'm a thin person. It's very strange. I mean, I have been fat almost my whole life, but I just click into thinking thin and thinking that I am thinner than I am. I get kind of surprised when I see myself. "Oh, I'm bigger than I thought I was."

Sarah summed it up when she said, "I'm deliberately choosing to have a smaller image of my physical body so that I can act out my idea of myself."

There is a paradox here: Large women who say they accept their body size also say they don't see themselves as large. For most women, body image is a fluid, mercurial, and changeable thing. It is shaped by all kinds of forces. These forces may come from the outside, such as a comment from a friend or stranger. They may come from the inside in the form of a feeling or observation about oneself. Or our image of our body may be shaped with time, as we confront images of ourself from the past, just as I did on Thanksgiving 1993.

> *Gale:* I still do not visualize myself accurately at 250 pounds. I have not mentally incorporated the weight gain of the past few years. I'm moving closer to that. I see myself as a large woman smaller than I am right now.

> *Sarah:* I am many images. I am not, and my body is not, this static, fixed thing. It changes depending on what my internal space is. It's not at all pathological; it's not about distortion. Perhaps it's about function or some inner play with how I am feeling.

Not everyone I talked to saw herself as smaller. Some women saw themselves as large as their mirrored reflection or photograph showed. They didn't hesitate to call themselves fat. They seemed to be able to use this word without the judgment that being large is bad or that being fat is something they had to change. There were also those who said they were proud to be a "woman of substance" or a "weighty woman" or one who felt empowered by her size. These women have what I call a transfigured body image. They have traveled through the territory of body-size acceptance and have come to a lifelike view of themselves. Marge said, "I look in the mirror every day and know that I am a large-size woman." Other women express it differently:

Joan: I have a mental picture of myself as being fat. I was about three or four when I realized that I was a fat kid. And I've never had any concept of myself other than fat.

Dianna: You know, without my clothes on my body looks like this: flat breasts hanging low, big hips, and big legs. I like to stand in front of the mirror and admire my big, strong body. I give myself a lot of support for who I am.

Having a body image that corresponds to body size seems to develop over time in the acceptance process. As we will see in chapter 6, "The Spiral of Acceptance," our body image may change as we change the degree of our self-acceptance. At first we may see ourself smaller than the mirrored or photographic image. This is the creative body image that allows us to act out our idea of ourself without being encumbered with fat stereotypes and helps us to move along the process of body-size acceptance. This may or may not lead to the transfigured body image. It really isn't important that you move from one type of body image to another. It's only important that you live the life you want in the body you have and that your body image helps you do this.

Finally, we need to ask ourselves different questions about body-image distortion. Is it really our body image that is distorted, or is it our belief about fat that is distorted? According to today's beliefs, if a woman is fat, she can't do certain things. She can't be smart or beautiful or creative or energetic. She can't have a life at all! But this is not the experience of women who have begun to be more size- and self-accepting. Our minds are too busy trying to put together our experience of being fat with the reality of our full lives. So we don't think of ourselves as fat in the same way that the woman who is on the other end of the weight continuum thinks of herself as fat. It's not so much an unrealistic body image as it's an unrealistic idea of what our experience of being fat is really like. The current stereotypes about fat people don't apply to us. They just don't fit. We've created a new vision of our body image and of being fat: We who are fat are not bad; we are just different.

Erin: Why would you want to have a fat body image even if you are fat? If you did, then you would have to act fat.

Ellen: Internally I have this image of a thinner person. I can do all these things. I experience myself as being able to move in the world, as being able to accomplish things, as being able to do normal stuff. So when I see myself in the mirror or in a picture, I say, "Geez, if I'm that fat, how can I do all these things?" Who knows how? I just do them.

Erin: When I started teaching aerobics, my husband said that I had been lied to, because even though I was always athletic, they told me I was fat. I always quit things because I was too embarrassed about my size. I have an athletic body, and when they told me I was fat, that was a lie.

Appreciating the diversity and beauty in all body types—valuing *difference*—is an important key to our self-acceptance. We need to stretch our minds to include images of beauty in women that are beyond the pages of *Vogue* and *Glamour.*

Not too long ago African-American beauty was not appreciated in our culture. African-American women who made it as finalists in beauty pageants were assimilated into the European-American version of beauty—lighter skin, straighter hair, smaller nose and lips. However, because of the conscious effort of African Americans during the 1960s and 1970s to reclaim their culture and their definition of beauty, the cultural ideals of what is beautiful have broadened to include images of African-American women—black *is* beautiful!

Likewise we larger women can begin to expand our vision and internal image of what is beautiful to include larger women with broader hips, fuller bellies and breasts, and rounder faces. We can do this by deliberately including images of beautiful large women in our daily life. This helps us to counteract the bombardment of thin images from TV, magazine covers, and billboards. Subscribing to *Radiance* can help. So can looking at women in the paintings of Renoir and Rubens and at Botero's sculptures. Look at the early goddess images, whose fuller bodies signified abundance, fertility, prosperity, and creativity. Look to nature as a reminder that the large, brilliant, hearty sunflower is as beautiful as the small, delicate, fragrant lily of the valley.

Body image is a complex idea. Some patterns, however, seem to apply consistently for larger women. First, our body image is fluid and changeable. It can change from day to day or from year to year whether we lose or gain a single pound. Second, we can adjust our body-image size to help us lead the high-quality life we want and deserve and in many cases have. Some of us see ourselves in the mirror and in our body image as fat women. Some of us have been able to adjust our ideas of what fat is and name ourselves as large or fat without negativity and without any pressure to change that part of ourselves.

Some studies endorse this revisioning of body image. One study that looked at the relationship between body image and depression, for instance, found that depressed college students were more dissatisfied with their bodies. Another reported that depressed individuals distorted their body image in a negative direction, while nondepressed individuals distorted their body image in an enhancing or positive manner. Sounds like the women with creative and transfigured body images to me! It also implies that doing this can help us fend off the depression we may feel about our body size.

Another study reports that the label a person assigns to her weight has consequences not only for her body image but also for her self-esteem. This means that those of us who have labeled our weight and size as positive (creative and transfigured versus "unrealistic") behave and think of ourselves in ways that can enhance our self-esteem. And enhancing our self-esteem enhances our lives.

What does all this have to do with you and me? These ideas relate to my story at the beginning of this chapter. At 135 pounds I was unhappy partly because I was still dissatisfied with my body and partly because I thought I was fatter than I actually was. Now, even though I weigh more, I feel better about myself because seeing myself smaller is really a re-creation of myself in my mind's eye. I go through my life seeing myself as a size sixteen, which allows me to do things I might not do if I really thought about what a size twenty-two woman ought to be doing. Remember my bathing suit story?

I do consider myself to be size-accepting. There are moments, however, when I am confronted with the fact that I am larger than I think I am. When I see photos of myself at this size, I get a glimpse of my old perception that I must be unattractive. Sometimes I even hate the reflection I see. Sometimes I feel sad about it. But then I breathe, put the photo away, and go on living my full life. My creative body image helps me to do that.

Let me be clear about another thing: Some of you may be thinking that this is denial—that it would be better to be more truthful and to see myself as I am. For years therapists have known about fat people's tendency to reduce their body image from large to small and have worked hard to get us to see ourselves "realistically." They do this because they think it's a great way to motivate us to diet. Having a smaller body image is indeed a kind of denial, but one that is healthy—a creative self-deception or a positive illusion. It's a tool to reclaim our lives. It works. And we know that dieting doesn't.

I am also aware that I may never have a transfigured body image. This doesn't mean I am less accepting of myself as a person. It's not important what we call our body image. It's more important to live life fully, day to day, without criticizing the body that takes us on our trip.

Christine summarized the elusiveness of body image. She's changed her mind to fit her body: "I used to think that this woman who teaches Jazzercise was just gorgeous, but she's not. It was a heart-stopping moment to look at her picture and think, 'Oh my God, she's stick thin,' and to recognize that this is not my ideal anymore. I don't want to look like that *ever*. That's a realization that I'm here, I've made it to where I want to be, with the recognition that there are many things I want to look like, but not like that."

Suggested Activities to Develop a Positive Body Image

PRACTICAL IDEAS

1. Begin to associate the word *big* with positive thoughts. For instance, people like to make "big money," work for a "big company," or "make it big" in the world. We like to think that we are bighearted. Being big is positive in many ways. Why can't it become a positive way to describe our bodies? Practice saying, "I'm big *and* beautiful."

2. Subscribe to *Radiance* and *Big Beautiful Woman* magazine. Having fashionable images of larger women around us can help change our idea of what is beautiful.

3. Find paintings of large women during various periods of art history and look at them often. This could be at the art museum or in books. Keep a favorite print of a larger woman someplace where she can remind you of her (and your) beauty.

4. Clean out your closet. Keep only those clothes that fit you now. Having five sizes of your former self staring at you from the closet every day can be terribly depressing.

5. Buy clothes that fit. Don't pay attention to size. Retailers will tell you that sizes change dramatically with different manufacturers. If the size bothers you, cut the label out. Go shopping with another large woman who will tell you the truth about the clothes you try on. Find a retailer you like and trust and have her dress you up.

JOURNAL ON THE FOLLOWING QUESTIONS

1. Remember a time in your life when you were thinner. What was happening in your relationships, work, family? Were there any moments in which you were *dissatisfied* with your life?

2. Now think about your life in your body today, the body that is larger than you'd like. What is happening in your relationships, work, family? Are there any moments in which you are *satisfied* with your life? What are they?

3. If you are thinking that your life was not all that great when you were thinner but that you *felt* better, consider this:

Did you feel better because everyone said you did ("Don't you feel better now that you've lost weight?")? Or because everyone said how great you looked being thinner? Or because you really did feel better? It's sometimes hard to separate how we really feel from how others tell us we should feel.

4. Are there any large women in your life whom you really like? Family members? Friends? Co-workers? Think about the qualities they have. Don't you like them for themselves? Isn't their weight irrelevant? Now reflect on your good qualities. Are you willing to consider yourself likable or lovable while being in a larger body? Are you willing to give yourself the same consideration that you give these other large women? Are you willing to like yourself for your good qualities regardless of your body size?

5. What type of body image do you have—creative or transfigured? How do you know? How do you feel about having a positive way to describe your body image experience?

WORKING WITH YOUR INNER BODY

1. Find photographs of yourself throughout various periods of your life. Line them up chronologically. Reflect on how you felt about your body during those different times—and why. Share these thoughts with a friend.

2. Find a picture of yourself when you were thinner. Look at it. Talk to the "you" of that time. Tell her that you're glad she was in your life. Tell her all the ways she helped you grow. Tell her you'll miss her, but you have to say good-bye. Let yourself feel the emotions that arise. Express these emotions in some way—by journaling, for instance, or sharing

them with a friend. Allow yourself the time to grieve the loss of your thinner body.

3. Use the visualizations in Hutchinson, *Transforming Body Image* (see "Recommended Reading"). (The visualizations are also available on audiotapes. Call the Crossing Press at 800-777-1048.)

4. Have a friend draw an outline of your body on a big sheet of paper. On the inside of your body outline, represent how you feel about your various body parts using the appropriate colors. Talk about it with your friend. Write about this experience in your journal.

5. With a friend take Polaroid photos of each other. Be playful. Take a variety of shots of your body—front, back, side, leaning over, lying down, and so on. Reflect on what you see and how you feel. Write in your journal or share with your friend.

6. Make up some affirmations about your body. Affirmations are positive statements about ourself that we say to ourself in order to counteract the effect of the critical voice inside us. An example of an affirmation is, "My body is the perfect size for me right now." Or "I like the roundness of my belly." See *Transforming Body Image* and *SomeBody to Love* for more ideas. Keep your affirmations where you can see them every day. Say them to yourself as often as possible.

7. When you have a creative body image, seeing photos or videos of yourself may bother you. My solution? Don't look at them! If looking at them upsets you, do the following: Breathe, then close your eyes and say one of your affirmations or remind yourself of your good qualities. Put the picture away. Go on with your day.

5

Spirit in Action:
Involvement in Something
Larger Than Ourself

I was once honored during women's history month with a community award for "contributing toward the personal and professional advancement of women." I was acknowledged publicly as a role model for women, especially as a large woman who works with size-esteem issues for all women. This is a portion of my acceptance speech for that award:

> Recently I was asked to describe my biggest vision for the world. I responded that I want to work for a world in which every human being is valued and honored for the gifts she or he brings—regardless of gender, ethnicity, race, or size. I feel committed to this idea because I have experienced what it is like to be a part of the out group looking in, first because I am a woman and second because I am a woman of size. A large woman. A woman who takes up space.

We hear a lot these days about acceptance of diversity in human beings, but people are referring primarily to ethnicity, race, and gender. I would like to add that acceptance of diversity in human beings related to appearance and size is also important. Millions of women in the world spend most of their day worrying about what they are or are not going to eat or how their bodies look or what they weigh. Women spend billions of dollars on diets and diet products. To this I say: What a waste of valuable, precious time, money, and resources. I ask you to ponder this: What might our country and world be like today if the time and energy women spend thinking about eating and body size were turned to solving the world's problems? And how far could those billions of dollars go toward feeding the hungry in this country instead of feeding the bank accounts of the diet industry?

So I stand here today being honored as a role model for women. I feel honored to be a part of the special group of women who have received this award before me. Each of us has brought her unique message to those women whose lives touch ours. My special message to the women in this audience today is this: If a woman of size, if you please, a "fat" woman like me, can have a successful, fulfilling life, then you can too. If a woman of size like me can be recognized and honored, then you can too. But you must reject the prejudices and stereotypes related to body-size and appearance standards because they are simply unattainable by most women.

Those of you who share this issue with me—fat, thin, or in-between—can decide to have a life in the body you already have. My wish for you is that you free up your time, energy, and resources to fight the real battles in this world instead of fighting yourself and your body.

We have been considering nondieting, size-accepting larger women from the perspective of self-concept and body image. A more complete picture of who we are includes exploring something else—our spirit. Spirit has been defined in many ways, but the "spirit" I am referring to here is the energy of connection we feel toward ourself and toward something larger than ourself. It is that which allows us to transcend the pain in our life in order to find some better experience or expression of our meaning.

The nondieting, size-accepting women I have talked to live in terms of connection and action. This comes through as a sense of personal spirituality and at times moves into "going public" as a fat woman. Being involved in something larger than ourself means having an active role in accepting a large body size—a positive surrendering to being both a larger woman and someone who has an interest in giving something back to the world. This connects us to the world in a way that is beyond our embodiment. Contrast this with women who passively give up on dieting but still wish for or obsess about being thinner. They are not positively connected to their bodies, and their preoccupation with appearance often leaves them with little energy for life's other pursuits.

This quality of spirit and action was noticeable in every woman I interviewed for my study and emerged in diverse ways and in varying degrees. I have noticed it in many women who have shared their size-acceptance stories with me. A woman who becomes active in accepting her body size is usually inspired by her personal definition of spirituality or her public declaration of size-acceptance, or both.

At the most basic level spirit in action means this: A larger woman recognizes and values the body in which she lives by taking care of it. She also realizes that she is more than her body. She has a mind and emotions and a creative life, which she also values. She spends time developing all of these parts of herself, seeking balance among them. Accepting her body's size and shape is part of her self-care and frees her to pay attention to the rest of her self and therefore the rest of her life. This often, but not always, is understood by the woman as a spiritual matter. And sometimes this attitude leads her into a more public sphere, with her spirit leading her body.

One quality of this spirit is that it can develop and change as our degree of size- and self-acceptance changes. In the earlier phases of body-size acceptance, we tend to be involved in this larger "something" that is more personal and private. We have a sense of connection in a spiritual way that is not easily defined but can be seen as related to the divine and/or nature.

Michelle: I can't define it well, but I have a sense of connectedness when I ask for help from something bigger than myself. I also need to feel a connection to women who need to express themselves. I think the power is there and that it is generated within. It leaves me searching.

Lois: Even if nobody else loves you, God loves you. And he doesn't care how much you weigh either. He loves skinny people too! My mother used to say that we're all the same in God's eyes. I think she was right.

Anne: I don't think God is aware that I'm over the insurance chart's weight limits.

Several women I talked to expressed their spirit by recognizing the diversity in nature reflected in the diversity in people.

Joan: When you're out in nature, one thing keeps repeating itself: Nothing is the same. Diversity is at the heart of God's plan. No two things are alike. The great big oak and the tiny sapling, every blade of grass, every snowflake—each is different. So if everything else in life can be different, why can't people? It makes the picture complete.

Some acknowledged their spirit through their connection with others who are also part of society's out group. Some did this in a more individual way, one to one, in their relationships with their families, friends, clients, or business contacts. In whatever form it's expressed, this private feeling of connection to something larger makes concerns about body size appear minor and insignificant.

As we larger women become more comfortable with our body size, this private sense of connection often expands to include giving something back to the world by going public as a fat woman. By this I mean that we are able to speak freely about our size publicly, without shame, in a way that (we hope) educates others.

Here are some examples of going public as a larger woman who is not ashamed of her body size: eating what you want when you want, even in public; letting people know that you don't appreciate fat jokes; ordering dessert in a restaurant; refusing to talk about diets when everyone else is; asking for a bigger chair or an armless chair at a family or public function; requesting a table that fits you in a restaurant and not squeezing yourself into a too-small booth just because the waiter puts you there; going to a public beach or pool and walking around in your bathing suit; asking the person next to you in the airplane if you can lift up the armrest to give you more room and comfort; wearing shorts in summer; letting the little kid in the shopping mall know that yes, you are a fat lady and that's because God made you big and made her small. Get the idea?

Once these kinds of actions become second nature to us, we can move, if we choose, to other levels of spirit in action: for instance, going public as role models or leaders for size acceptance. Many large women quietly become role models by living their lives fully but in ways that are not directly related to promoting body-size acceptance. Living the life they want in the body they already have allows them to affect positively other large women. Whether being a role model was intentional or not, this lifestyle involves them in something larger than themselves.

Joy: After I give my programs about positive self-image, I am approached by all kinds of women, but I feel especially good when the larger women come up to talk to me. It's like being a kindred spirit— "I know how you feel," "I'm here for you," and "There's another way." I'm thrilled to be able to make that kind of difference.

Dianna: Being a role model? I think that's happened a lot in my experience as teacher and lecturer. People see my self-acceptance and admire it.

Many of the women I talked to are in leadership roles in the arena of size-acceptance. They're doing things such as organizing aerobics classes for larger women, participating in groups such as NAAFA (the National Association to Advance Fat Acceptance), teaching courses and leading workshops related to size-acceptance, and working in the large-size clothing industry. Pat Lyons, coauthor of *Great Shape: The First Fitness Guide for Large Women,* takes her leadership role in the size-acceptance movement seriously when she refers to herself as a "professional fat person." All of these actions (and others I haven't mentioned here) take the original stigma of being fat and transform it into something worthwhile and meaningful for large women and the culture. These actions change the person who is doing them, the people around her, and the environment in which she lives.

Christine: Society is going to change only when we start saying that we deserve better treatment. When we started the exercise class, we took a public stance that proclaimed that we deserve good things too. There's also an element of breaking new ground, of making a place for us.

Acting as a leader goes against society's biased view of us, thereby allowing us once again to defy the stereotypes of fat people. After all, society believes that fatness is controllable, so anyone who is fat is publicly exhibiting flaws in her basic nature. Right? Wrong! Size-accepting fat women who have gone public as leaders speak and act as if they have a right to be heard. This sends a powerful message to the world: You can't shame me anymore!

Being a leader or a role model for size-acceptance brings us into the sphere that allows us to see the bigger picture of who we are and what we have to give back to the world. It helps us define our purpose in life, which is to have a set of values and concepts that make life meaningful. Purpose is the notion of directing one's energy toward personally relevant goals, making life fuller, richer, and more worthwhile.

A larger woman who is putting her spirit into action is probably saying these kinds of things to herself: "I am a large woman in spirit as well as body. I have been shamed and hurt because of my size, so I know what it's like to be considered different. I am a good person who hasn't harmed anyone, and I don't deserve to be treated this way. Neither do other large women. I refuse to take the shame the world puts on me and others like me. I intend to live my life fully, doing what I can to care for myself and others." This kind of attitude is spiritually grounded and launches a woman into being something larger than herself, which ultimately nourishes her soul.

Dieting and body hate, by contrast, take this energy and turn it into a narcissistic obsession with having the perfect body. Ask any woman who has been there and she'll tell you that there's barely room for anything else in her life. Even when she does accomplish work or personal goals, it is often tainted with that unremitting sense of not being good enough because of her body. Or worse, her accomplishments take second place to her ultimate goal of losing weight.

The Role of Support

How does a woman achieve the size- and self-acceptance that can launch her into something larger than herself, that can free her spirit into action and connection? The answer is in one word: *support!* I cannot overemphasize the importance of support in this process. Every single woman I've ever talked to about size-acceptance has had support for changing her mind about her body.

A number of studies confirm the importance of support for people who are going through a life transition. For example, one study showed that isolation (which is the opposite of support) can lead to illness, whereas developing a connection to others (support) can promote health. The social prejudice against fat people creates an environment of isolation that can be a source of stress. People who experience stress in isolation are at a greater risk for both physical and psychological problems. Because of this, being supported and giving support back to other large people allow us to develop a connection, thereby easing our feelings of isolation and their accompanying stress. This in turn gives us more energy to devote to involvement in something larger than ourself.

The role of support often changes while we are going through our process of building size-esteem. At first it is crucial to receive support for who we are in the body we already have. This entails focusing on the things we can do and do well regardless of size. It also means focusing on being OK in a larger body. This support can come in many different forms—relationships, books and research on fat and body image, the large-size clothing industry, NAAFA or other groups of size-accepting people, feminism, or personal spirituality.

Anne: As a youngster I felt very nurtured. My grandmother used to say to me, "Oh, you have such good flesh!" She was wonderful.

Lois: If you ask my kids if they would rather have a fat mom or a skinny mom, they'll say, "A fat mom!" They tell me that they like my nice lap, all cuddly and comfortable.

Dianna: My self-acceptance as a fat woman began when I first associated with feminists. It was empowering not to feel discriminated against because I was fat.

Christine: Reading *Radiance* and *BBW* has supported me by reinforcing the concept that you can be large and beautiful.

Later, when we are feeling more size-esteem and self-acceptance, getting support transforms into giving support. This happens because we are seen, with or without our awareness, as role models for other larger women.

Michelle: My experience is that it is absolutely necessary to have the support. Working with other large women was a very positive experience in that we were role models for one another.

One reward for giving support to others is the incremental way this works to change our culture's attitudes about fat people. This change in attitude in turn works to support us. For instance, I often tell my students that I am teaching the class on self-esteem not only to help these larger women develop a healthier attitude about themselves but also to help me, because every convert to size-acceptance makes my life easier. I have one less person to convince that my worth is not dependent on my body size.

Another example is my story at the beginning of this chapter. Being given an award for my work with women, especially in the area of body image, gave me the opportunity to be public about being a fat woman who also has a life. This kind of event in the life of any large woman sends a strong message to everyone watching: It supports other large women in having a life in the body they already have; it shows women who "feel fat" that being thin isn't everything; and it educates the rest that fat people do not fit the stereotypes. Marcia Hutchinson calls this process "the ripple [that] becomes a wave and finally a tide which cannot be ignored."

I hope you will feel inspired to do several things. First, examine how your size fits in with your definition of personal spirituality. In other words, how can you connect with yourself, your "spirit," in positive, affirming, and self-loving ways? How can you connect with others in ways that will express your spirit? Then wait and watch for your spirit to move you to action, to encourage you to become involved in the world in ways that are larger than your personal concerns about your body size. Then do it! And seek support for the essence of who you are. After all, you have a body, but you are more than your body. Express the "more" of you. And experience how your spirit in action magically transforms your life into something larger than yourself.

Suggested Activities to Develop Your Spirit in Action

PRACTICAL IDEAS

1. Develop your support network. This can be done in a variety of ways. Read *Radiance* and *BBW* along with any other books and articles that support a size-acceptance point of view. Talk to a trusted friend or family member, and ask them to support you in your new perspective. Find a group of women, meet regularly, and share your experiences of this process. Take a class on size-esteem, or go on a retreat for larger women. Join NAAFA. Go clothes shopping with a larger woman friend.

2. Become active in areas of your life that do not revolve around body size, food, or dieting obsessions—such as community, church, or volunteer work.

3. Take a movement class that emphasizes a size-acceptance, nondieting approach for larger women. If there is none in your neighborhood, go to your local Y or community center and help organize one.

4. Discover one way you enjoy being creative. Use the watercolors or paints that have been sitting in the closet over the years. Or try other methods of artistic expression. You

may want to elevate your role as family cook to gourmet chef. Write the short story or poem you've been putting off. Sing in the shower or dance to your favorite music. Garden or create your own special place in your home where you can meditate, read, or just be quiet. However your creativity desires to be expressed, make room and time in your life to work out your creative muscle.

5. Make a list of the ways in which you can "go public" about being a larger woman. Is this with friends or family members, your physician or therapist? Is it by asking a thinner friend to go shopping with you at a large-size clothing store without feeling like you've asked her for a huge favor? You might go public by letting it be known that you no longer believe dieting is the healthiest activity for you or by not participating in diet talk at home or at work. Prioritize your list by putting the least risky idea at the top. When you feel ready, do the first one. Work your way down the list.

6. Go for a walk or a ride in a "nature-ific" area. Notice the diversity in the ways things look and grow. Imagine this spot being all the same color or filled with the same flowers or exactly the same rocks. Take a moment to appreciate the differentness in everything and how one thing's beauty does not distract from the beauty of the other things around it. Each complements the other.

JOURNAL ON THE FOLLOWING QUESTIONS

1. Think about your personal definition of "spirit" or "spirituality." Is this defined as God? Goddess? Or by your

religion? Is this your creative spirit, or your intuition? What is spirit to you? Write down your thoughts about this.

2. Now try to connect your sense of spirit or spirituality to your personal experiences of living in a larger body. What comes to you about this connection?

3. Reflect on the affirmation "I have a body, but I am more than my body." What does this mean to you?

4. Think about the times in your life when you have gone public as a larger woman. Write about these experiences. How did it feel to do this? If you were to do them again today, how might they be different because you are different?

5. Write about the support you need in your process of building size-esteem. Who are the people who can help? How can they help? Why is it important for these particular people to be on your side about this?

6. Have you ever been honored for something you've done? Or won an award? Or been given some kind of public recognition? Write about this and include your honest feelings about this recognition. Did you feel you deserved it? Did your feelings about your body play into how worthy you felt to receive this award?

7. Think about the times you have given something back to the world through your actions. How did you feel? Did you spend any time thinking about your body size?

8. Reflect on the occasions when you didn't think about your body while you were doing something. What were you doing? Try to remember what it was like to be lost in an activity where you were free from obsessive thoughts about your size. Imagine what it would be like to feel this way all the time.

Part Three

A Guide to Sane Living

6

The Spiral of Acceptance

The lights are hot and bright. I'm wondering what I'm doing here, on stage, in front of this audience. I feel nervous. My mouth is dry, my pulse is racing, and I'm trying to remember to breathe. I look around to make contact with faces in the audience. Some look at me and smile. I smile back. Those smiles help me feel a bit more reassured and connected to what is about to happen.

Gradually I lose my nervousness about being on national TV debating a fat-phobic physician because I am getting mad! I'm trying to defend two little girls' right to stay in their home with their family—even if they are fat. The physician continues to spout stereotypes about being fat, including one I haven't heard before—being denied the "joy of sex." (As if this were relevant to a six- and a ten-year-old girl!) I'm clearly in touch with my five-year-old self, the one who was sent away from home for being fat. "Don't let this happen again!" she whispers to me. So with her support and my expert status as doctor, I am brave enough to speak my truth along with research that clearly contradicts what the physician is saying. He obviously isn't prepared to debate someone who has the information I do, so he quits spewing fat stereotypes and begins to attack me instead: "You're obese," he says. "We can only hope you don't drop dead from your obesity right here on stage."

He drops this bomb in a last-ditch effort to discredit me. It doesn't matter that I have out-researched him, and it doesn't matter that he can't adequately defend the action he is condoning. He reduces our intellectual debate into a petty attack on me based on my body size. Because I am fat, I am fair game to him—just like those two girls he is trying to get removed from their home because they too are fat.

I hear what he says, but it takes a moment to hear what he really means. I check on my five-year-old self. She is a little shaken, but she's not broken. Being who I am, I rise to the occasion and shake off what he has said to me like I'm shaking off a pesky mosquito. I don't buckle. I don't wince. And, most important, I don't hurt! I think he's acting ridiculous, and I know he's just made a fool of himself on national TV. His insult makes me feel stronger because I realize that I have won this debate—and that he, although thin, is ridiculous, whereas I, although fat, am smart.

I tell this particular story to begin discussing what I call the spiral of acceptance because it illustrates one of the most important qualities of size-acceptance: It is a process. Being on that TV stage as an adult debating an action that profoundly affected me as a child integrated those two parts of me by combining experience with wisdom, and intellect with feeling. I could not have done that earlier in my process of size- and self-acceptance. I might have been able to recite research studies, but I never would have left that stage unscathed by his comment, which essentially meant "Drop dead, fatso." At another time in my process of self-acceptance I would probably have translated that comment into shame. It would have been like being made fun of in front of a third-grade classroom by someone saying, "Fatty, fatty, two by four. . . . " But not now. Now when someone tries to shame me, I get mad. What has made the difference is my process—what I personally, as a larger woman, have been sorting through for years.

What does *process* mean? The dictionary defines it as "a series of actions, changes or functions that bring about an action or an end result; the course or passage of time; ongoing movement, progression." Using this definition as our base, we can explain the process of body-size acceptance as ongoing movement over time that brings about the result of accepting and caring for ourselves in the bodies we already have. The key words are "ongoing movement over time." I've said it before, and I'm saying it again: This stuff takes time.

But how do we know we are accepting our body just as it is? Does accepting our body mean that we can never change it (or ourselves) in some way? The answers vary, based on our individual values of time and money, standards of appearance, concerns about health, life pursuits, family background, and available energy.

In other words, body-size acceptance is a personal decision, as well it should be. If someone comes along and tells
you in absolute terms what constitutes a size-accepting
woman, run for the hills! That's just as bad as the diet industry telling you what your body should look like. Both deny
your individual choice and your responsibility for your body,
its appearance, its health, and its connection to you. Remember your "body's truths"? Your body's size and the ways
you accept and care for your body are two of them.

My own bottom-line definition of body-size acceptance
resides in the act of not dieting. I believe that if I'm dieting
for weight loss, I'm not accepting my body as it is. Dieting
seems to be an out-of-sync way to relate to my body, a way to
deny, control, and abuse it (do you get the feeling that I'm
definitely against dieting?). This is the main reason I interviewed only nondieting fat women for my research study,
which I undertook as part of my doctoral work.

In addition to a nondieting lifestyle, other criteria for
body-size acceptance had to be defined, at least initially, for
my study. I decided that the women I wanted to interview
had to be at least thirty years old, because I believe that we
are inclined to be more accepting of ourselves as we age.
The women also had to be "moderately to severely overweight" (someone else's terms), which is defined as at least
40 percent over the ideal weights listed on the height-weight
chart. I chose this weight range because I wanted to talk to
women who actually were fat by society's standards. They are
the ones who have to face the social stigma every day. And if
they could figure out how to accept themselves and live large
in the world, then any woman could! Finally, the women I in-

terviewed had to consider themselves size-accepting and to believe they led a meaningful and well-adjusted life.

The kind of study I did is called phenomenological. This approach to research does not use a number system to define reality. For instance, I didn't test these women to measure if they were size-accepting—I took their word for it. In this kind of research, reality (or phenomenon) is defined by the subjects themselves as they report it to the researcher. This is important for you to know because the process of acceptance that I outline in this chapter comes directly from the experiences of these particular fat women and not from someone else's (outside the "fat worldview") interpretations of their experience. And since I consider myself to be a size-accepting fat woman who has lived, suffered, studied, and felt the joys of being larger, I am also a part of this group. This gives me a valid perspective from which to interpret these (our) experiences.

Your experiences of body-size acceptance may be different from those I describe here. The spiral of acceptance I examine in this chapter is intended to guide you through the territory of size- and self-acceptance and is not the final word on your process. Use it as a tool, keep what works for you, and throw out the rest. You don't need another "expert" to tell you how to live your life. You are the expert on your life.

When I interviewed the women who met my basic guidelines as size-accepting women, I was challenged to go even farther in defining and understanding what "acceptance" really means for us. For instance, all the women in my study said they accepted their weight and size, yet some seemed more accepting than others. In order to make sense of this

I began to imagine each woman on a continuum of acceptance. Without judging one position on this continuum as
being better than another (all the women were in the territory of size-acceptance), I was able to clarify some behaviors
and attitudes that are subject to change as we go through
this complex process.

Another challenge for me was to try to picture this process. These women's stories of acceptance didn't move in a
straight line, so I couldn't say they were stages. Instead their
stories had a fluid quality, a circular movement, going back
and forth, never regressing but sometimes revisiting old behavior before they transformed it or gave it up completely.
This movement reminded me of a spiral shape, moving in
circles, flowing upward or deepening downward. Sometimes,
therefore, it may seem as though we've come to a place
we've been before, but we really haven't. And sometimes we
may feel as if we're going around in circles, but we really
aren't. We're just looking at ourselves and our process from
a different perspective—from a higher or deeper place.
Often (as contradictory as this may seem) the way up and
the way down are the same: As we move down, sinking into
our process of size-acceptance, something significant often
rises to the surface. Moving within the spiral is a place of discovery that usually begins with no known goal in mind and
no place to "get to," as if this were a journey with a destination. As one woman said, "I don't feel in control of where I
am going to end up."

It's no wonder this woman doesn't know where she's
going to end up. None of us really does. For the most part
we've been making it up as we go—and anyplace is better

than the body-obsessed place we've been in. There have been very few role models to show us the way—larger women who are successful in the public sphere who don't apologize for or act ashamed of their bodies. So instead we've been using our intuition, personal experiences, and support to move us along our way.

What are these behaviors and attitudes that change and transform us as we move within the spiral of acceptance? I uncovered six indicators through my interviews. How we "do food" is one of them—compulsive eating and dieting behavior. Another is our body image, whether viewed as creative or transfigured. Deciding to live in the present rather than in the past or future is the third. Fourth is living an inner-determining lifestyle. Support is fifth. Sixth is becoming involved in something larger than ourselves. Do any of these sound familiar? Only everything we've been discussing so far in *Nothing to Lose!*

If these are the behaviors and attitudes that change while we go through the process of size-acceptance, then what are the guideposts we can refer to as the markers of our process? I've mapped these places within the spiral of acceptance based on their position to one another and named them as such: preacceptance, initial acceptance, midpoint acceptance, and decisive acceptance. (As you can see, there are more words to describe a linear process than a spiraling one. Just think of these as signposts, footprints, map points, or crumbs of bread left along the trail.)

Let's take a closer look at each of the places within the spiral of acceptance to see what we can learn about this process and how we can relate to it personally.

Preacceptance

Preacceptance is a time when a woman is feeling ambivalent and passive about being large. She may give up on her body size and weight, which is something different from the positive surrendering we discussed earlier. This woman is not dieting, yet she thinks she will probably diet again sometime in her life.

> *Carla:* I would be delighted to weigh 150 pounds, but I won't do any dieting to get there. It takes too much energy. Yet I think that I would have more energy if I lost weight.

Preacceptance usually indicates unfamiliarity with the current research that supports a "fat can be healthy/fit/ happy" attitude. The woman in this place on the spiral does not like being fat. She doesn't like other fat people very much either, since she believes some of the cultural stereotypes about fat people. She lacks a support system, and because of this she could be persuaded to go on another diet. Or she could spiral into initial acceptance.

Initial Acceptance

Initial acceptance is the first place a larger woman shows active acceptance of body size and a positive surrendering to her body's truths: "I am a larger woman, and given my dieting history, I will probably always be. Now what?" This woman no longer sees dieting as a viable option; but because she has been a chronic dieter, she probably, and understandably, still has some issues around food and eating. She begins the process of learning to trust herself with food by trying not to control her eating through dieting. She also stops weighing herself and using the scale as a measure of her self-worth.

> *Erin:* When I decided I'd never diet again, I threw out my scale. That was hard. Now I know I can accept myself at this weight for the rest of my life and it wouldn't bother me. But I can't accept how I'm still eating compulsively.

The creative body image is part of initial acceptance. Remember, creative body image is when a woman sees herself as smaller than her mirrored or photographed reflection. Having a creative body image has a positive effect in the woman's life because it allows her to act out her idea of herself unencumbered by the fat stigma.

Because of her creative body image, a woman who is initially accepting of her size is able to live more fully in the present rather than living for a time when she'll be thinner. Since dieting and weight loss are no longer options, she begins to do things she was postponing until she lost weight. Thus she begins to accumulate evidence that she can have the life she wants in the body she already has, right now, even at her size.

> *Christine:* The first time someone asked me what I would do with my life if I never lost weight, I thought, "Am I supposed to have a life besides dieting?" So I sat down

and listed the things that would make me happy and what I want out of life. I realized that thinness wasn't going to give me any of these things and that I had a lot of them already.

Not dieting, throwing out the scale, having a creative body image, and living for the present help build a strong base for moving from being what the culture says she should be as a fat person to being who she wants to be as a person—regardless of weight. This reinforces her inner-determining lifestyle, because she listens to her own inner voice rather than the collective voice of the culture.

Sarah: When I was about thirty, weight and dieting were still important to me. In the last ten years I've been slowly claiming back the importance of me and not letting the weight be the central issue.

During initial acceptance (as with the other places in the spiral), support becomes central to the continuation of her process. Doing research on the failure of dieting, reading fat-positive literature, sharing her decision to become size-accepting, and relying on friends and relatives to give her positive feedback about who she is (besides being fat) are all a part of her support network.

Midpoint Acceptance

The midpoint place in the spiral of acceptance is characterized by being in the middle (obviously) of initial and decisive acceptance. Here active acceptance is amplified through more outward activity. Dieting and scales are definitely out. Any eating issues left over from chronic dieting are no longer experienced and labeled as compulsive. Instead a woman here moves toward healthful eating: How she eats and moves her body are now seen as lifestyle changes for health rather than ways to lose weight. This helps her feel more in control of these parts of her life, which formerly felt out of control.

> *Sarah:* My health issues put into focus that it doesn't really matter what I look like or what I weigh. What really matters is how all my body parts work and how my body has served me in some wonderful ways.

The creative body image continues to have meaning at midpoint acceptance because a woman still sees herself smaller than she is yet larger than what society says is acceptable. For instance, she may be a size twenty-four yet see herself as a size eighteen, which is still large in a culture that prefers women to be a size six or eight. She now allows herself a body-image perception that is closer to her actual size.

> *Sarah:* I still don't visualize myself at 250 pounds. I see myself closer to 180 pounds.

Living a greater portion of her life in the present allows her to accumulate even more evidence of her worth. Her attitude is "I don't have to wait to get thin to have the things I want in my life." This allows her to be more assertive about her body when confronted by the culture.

> *Abby:* I told my boyfriend, "You must accept me just as I am right now, at this weight, or it's over. I'm not letting this become an issue, because I've had it with this being an issue."

Midpoint in the spiral is the place where she is more consistent in listening to her inner voice, leading a more inner-determining lifestyle. Trust in her body truths grows, and she accumulates more evidence of her worth. Her support network helps immensely. And finally she becomes involved in something larger than herself (whether or not she wants to) because now she is a visible role model for other women of size. Because she is living without dieting—indeed because she *has a life*—other people notice.

> *Michelle:* What happened was that I had the practical experience of being in my body, of being out there. Doing professional dance, performing in one way or another, makes it easier for me to do the other things I want to do in my life.

Decisive Acceptance

Decisive acceptance is the final place in the spiral. It is characterized by explicit action related to size-esteem. Being decisive means that a woman has taken the power to determine what her size means to her, regardless of what the culture says. She publicly displays her decision to accept that which is unacceptable to the rest of society—her large, fleshy, fat, taking-up-space-with-no-apologies body.

Dianna: This is my fat and I like it!

She also has determination. No one gets to her about her weight, because she says in essence, "I'm fat. It's OK that I'm fat. I have a full, rewarding life being fat. If being fat is so awful, how do you explain me?" She has transcended the public misconceptions of fat women by the reality of her full life.

Christine: I began to recognize that all of us, regardless of size, are human beings. So when we put together the brochure for our exercise class, we included our pictures. We made a public statement, a kind of declaration of, "Here we are! We're human beings too, and I dare you to say anything about our weight!"

Another noticeable result of decisive acceptance is the absence of a fixation on food or eating. Some women I interviewed never even mentioned food and eating. These were nonissues, presumably because these women had reconnected to their hunger in their own individual way. In other words, they had stabilized their relationship with food. At this stage, nondieting behavior is fully integrated into a woman's lifestyle.

In decisive acceptance, body-image perception is usually the transfigured type rather than the creative type. A woman with a transfigured body image sees herself as she is and interprets her larger size as something positive, even desirable.

She appears to have integrated her sense of herself as being larger, which does not get in her way of having a life. In fact, being larger is often seen as enhancing her life because of the decisive stand she has taken about it.

> *Joan:* I'm short, fat, blond, blue-eyed, and fair-skinned. To imagine myself as thin would be the same as trying to imagine myself five-feet eight, with dark hair, brown eyes, and an auburn complexion. That would be somebody else. It wouldn't be me.

Living in the present continues to be important, along with recognizing past accomplishments and working toward future goals. None of her plans is contingent upon her body size. From a well-established base of deciding and acting from her inner voice, she moves back into the culture in a more public way as a leader or role model for size-acceptance. This is the going-public piece of being involved in something larger than herself. By supporting a change of attitude in the culture, she is also supporting herself.

> *Joy:* My choice of profession [image consultant] has had an impact on my own size-acceptance. It's been a part of the transition for me, because the more I do this, the more it reinforces accepting myself.

So there you have it—the spiral of body-size acceptance with its particular behaviors and attitudes. Did you recognize yourself in any of these places? Did anything resonate as you read about particular experiences? Or did you feel confused, saying, "Yes, yes!" at one moment, then "No way!" the next? Or "Here's where I am" only to then read about a behavior or attitude that is definitely not yours? These responses are the pitfalls of trying to describe a process that does not move in a straight line. Your process is affected by your age, developmental tasks for your age, time, motivating factors, and so on. This is what makes it an individual approach and not a general prescription for everyone to follow, step-by-step. So if you see some of your behaviors in the midpoint place and others in the initial place, and maybe even a decisive acceptance attitude thrown in for good measure, then yes, you're there! *Remember, it doesn't matter where you are within the spiral of acceptance. It matters only that you have entered its realm with a willingness to have the life you want in the body you already have.*

One woman I interviewed summarized her process of body-size acceptance in this way:

Michelle: I used to view myself as though the fat were something separate. It was as though I was the person inside the fat as opposed to my flesh being a part of me. You know the old cliché, "There's a thin person inside every fat person." But the truth is that a fat person is a person too. Gradually over the years I've come to own the fat on top of my muscles. This makes it easier to accept *all* of me. I'm a whole person these days, integrated.

How to Move Through the Spiral of Acceptance

Given what we have just learned about the spiraling process of body-size acceptance, there is one more lesson the women I interviewed can teach us: *how* they moved through the spiral of acceptance. In other words, what methods did they use to keep on the size-acceptance track? The most obvious way, which we've already addressed, is support, the kind that comes mainly from outside sources, such as books, friends, and therapists.

In addition to having outside support, there were three distinct tactics these women used as internal support: positive self-talk, reframing, and acting as if. Let's go through each one of these terms, which derive from the counseling profession, to see what they offer.

Positive self-talk is a way to undermine the negative messages we get from ourselves and others. You know what I mean—the constant, critical voice inside our head that keeps saying how ugly, dumb, awful, and unlovable we are. Positive self-talk replaces the negative messages with, obviously, positive ones. In theory the more we give ourselves positive messages, the more positively we will view ourselves, thereby improving our self-esteem. The women I talked to were able to employ this strategy because someone (such as a therapist) suggested it or they had read about it or they naturally figured out that the voice in their head was making a big difference in the quality of their life.

Christine: Language and the way in which I speak to myself are important. As far as my size-acceptance is concerned, there have been some profound ways in which I speak to myself. It started out as this little voice of criticism going on all day. Now it's the little friend inside me who keeps me going when I need it. It's a heck of a lot easier to live this way.

Reframing is another strategy these women used, often as a natural response to the negative messages of the culture. Reframing means taking an idea we see in one way and changing it by changing our perception of it in a way that enhances our purposes. Reframing is a matter of changing perceptions or changing "frames," turning a culturally negative perception into one that is individually positive.

Erin: When you couple exercise with weight loss, you devalue the exercise. Exercise is in fact something you do to feel good and not because you want to lose weight.

Sarah: The concept of big in my family is that all of the women who are big are also healthy and strong. So now the association with being big is also with health and strength rather than with sickness or weakness.

Joan: There's a sensation, a sway to my body, that's almost like a pendulum. It's an independent force due to my size. It's fun. There's a kind of "jiggle-osity" to it.

Acting as if is a way of acting and behaving in practice the way we would want to if we actually possessed the qualities (or body) we desire. Acting as if means that we don't have to be slaves to our ever-changing emotions around our physiology. We can practice behaving as our ideal self in our day-to-day lives. This gives us the experiences we desire but don't think we deserve because of our size. Once we act as if we have a right to do certain things, we learn that we actually can do them, which keeps us doing more and more. For instance, the creative body image is one way of acting as if—I'm acting as if I were a size ten, which allows me to move through the world as a size ten, which gets me what a size ten woman has. If I can have what I want by pretending to be a size ten, why can't I let myself have what I want in my size eighteen body?

Michelle: So much of it, especially in the beginning, was acting as if I could be certain ways. And the more I did this, the more I realized that I could have whatever I wanted.

Christine: It took a full measure of courage to walk out in a leotard into a room full of strangers and have someone take my picture and put it in a newspaper. I think I made a public statement about my size and my right to exercise long before I really felt that way. It's as if a part of me did this and pulled the rest of me along. So if I put it out there, then maybe I'd *have* to be that way.

Positive self-talk, reframing, and acting as if allowed the women I interviewed to work continually toward the goal of accepting their bodies, which initiated a series of changes in their feelings about their bodies. As I mentioned earlier, some said they had no specific goal in mind when they began to think about body-size acceptance. They weren't

sure where they were heading—except away from struggling with their bodies. They had tried everything in order
to conform to the social pressure of having the perfect
body, yet nothing they did provided a permanent solution.
The skills of talking to themselves positively, reconstructing
their thoughts and perceptions, and practicing their ideal
behavior became some of the most important ways they
learned to find their way out of body hate and to accept
their body size.

When I began this research, I was sure I would uncover
the one true process women went through to size-esteem. I
realize now, however, that the spiral of acceptance is just
one way to conceptualize our process. More ways exist, because, as I keep saying, this is a complex matter. We can of
course share our experiences with one another, but ultimately we will have to live our own way through it—slowly
and gradually.

Dianna: I don't think of myself on a journey to self-
acceptance. Rather I would say that I have accepted myself to different degrees and different dimensions for
much of the last twenty-five years of my life. When I think
of a journey, I think of a more linear route and a definite
destination. I haven't known what the destination is for
me, so it's been more a process of discovery: Let's see
what happens on my travels in my body. I didn't set out
for this, but it has been a wonderful place to be and to
keep going toward. I could say the same things to you
now that I might have said to you ten years ago, and they
would have been true both times. But now I experience

them at a much deeper level of my being. I just know deeply that I trust my body.

What can you do to begin this process of acceptance or, if you have begun, to hasten it along? Start now by taking a deep breath. Begin talking to yourself about yourself in the most positive ways. Breathe. Learn to see the world *through* your body size, not in *spite* of it. Breathe. Now act as if you have a right to your life in the body you already have. Breathe. Be patient. Soon you will find yourself moving through your own personal version of the spiraling territory of self-acceptance and size-esteem.

Suggested Activities for Moving Through the Spiral of Acceptance

PRACTICAL IDEAS

1. Look around for a larger woman whom you admire. This could be someone you know—a family member or a friend. Or it could be someone who is more well known, such as Carol Shaw, founder of *BBW* magazine, the actresses Kathy Najimy, Kathy Bates, the opera singer Marilyn Horne, or the writer Clarissa Pinkola Estés. Whenever you think about this person, remind yourself that she is a larger woman who has done well with her life regardless of her weight. Think about her often as a role model for you.

2. Get a long sheet of paper and some pens or crayons. Make your lifeline on the paper, beginning with your birth and continuing to where you are now, leaving more room at the end of the paper so that you can add to it every so often.

Mark your lifeline with your important life events and life-changing decisions. Then go through it again and record your weight history—the ups and downs of the scale and your feelings about your weight. Once you finish your lifeline, take a long look at it. Think about it. Do you see any relationship between certain life events and your body weight? Can you draw any conclusions about your own process of body-size acceptance from your lifeline?

3. Draw a map of the spiral of acceptance as I've described it. Be creative with how you visualize it and where you see yourself within it. Mark those places that are meaningful to you with a symbol, such as a star, an exclamation point, a cross, or a check mark. Study it to understand what your attitudes and behaviors related to size-acceptance are right now. Refer to your spiral occasionally to check in with your process.

4. If you are in the preacceptance place in the spiral of acceptance, think about what you can do to move into initial acceptance. It could be not weighing yourself everyday or putting your scale away or eating without dieting. You might start by reading more research about how fat can be fit or by making friends with a larger woman. Think of other things you could do and list them. Commit yourself to do at least one item on your list today. Refer to your list often to see what other action you can do to spiral your process into initial body-size acceptance.

5. If you are in the initial place of body-size acceptance, think about what you can do to move into midpoint acceptance. For instance, you could throw away your scale or learn to eat for your health. You could move your body for the

sheer pleasure of it, not for weight loss. You could recognize your creative body image as one that works for you and act as if you were the size you see yourself as. Think of other things you could do and list them. Commit yourself to do at least one item on your list today. Refer to your list often to see what other action you can do to spiral your process into midpoint acceptance.

6. If you are midpoint in your process of body-size acceptance, think about what you can do to move toward decisive acceptance. It could be eating for health *and* pleasure because you trust your body's truths about food or allowing yourself to become more comfortable with photographs of yourself or continuing to make decisions about your life in the present and to act on them, regardless of your weight. List other things and commit yourself to do at least one item on your list today. Refer to your list often to see what other action you can do to spiral your process into decisive acceptance.

7. If you are decisive about accepting your body size, think about what you can do to reinforce your process. You might wish to recognize yourself as a role model for other larger women and to begin to mentor them into their own acceptance. You could go public as a size-accepting woman at work or take on leadership for this issue within NAAFA or your own community. You could write or speak on size-esteem. Commit yourself to continuing and strengthening your process of living your rich, full life in the body you already have.

8. Practice positive self-talk in this way: Make a list of all the things you have ever done of which you are proud. It

doesn't have to be earth-shattering stuff, just things that you know are accomplishments for you. It could be taking a speech class even though you were terrified or cooking the best lasagna on the block when you couldn't boil water two years ago. Perhaps you are the most active parent in your PTA or have gone back to school.

Every day, or at least every week, add items to your list. Keep this list by your bedside, and read it as often as possible—at least once a day. This helps to change the grooves in your brain to include these positive thoughts about yourself. Read them until you become comfortable with hearing these things and knowing these things about yourself. This is not egotistical or self-centered or boastful. It is gathering factual information and building awareness about the things you can do well.

This list is the evidence you can bring out when your negative, critical voice begins talking to you. This list will allow you to counter its negative message with your positive voice, which says you are active, ambitious, bright, creative, talented, and _____ (fill in the blank).

9. Practice reframing this way: Think of all the messages the culture has sent you about being larger. Things such as, I have to exercise to lose weight; being fat means being unhealthy; my body is fat and therefore unlovable. Now put a different, personal twist on your thoughts, such as, I want to exercise because it feels good; being fat means being strong enough to withstand some health problems; my larger body is soft, warm, cuddly, and desirable. Notice how the culture has taught you to construct the idea of fat, and reconstruct it for yourself in a personally positive way.

10. Practice acting as if in this way: Go to an exercise class and act as if you have the right to be there. Put on a bathing suit or shorts and act as if you were a smaller size and go for a swim or a walk. Go to a party and act as if you were the most attractive woman there, and talk to a new person. Go into a lingerie shop for larger women, buy a new teddy, and go home and act as if you were the sexiest person your partner has ever been with. Get the idea? Act as if you have a right to the life you want in the body you already have.

JOURNAL ON THE FOLLOWING QUESTIONS

1. When was the first time you heard the idea that you didn't have to lose weight to be OK? How did you feel about this idea when you first heard it? How does this idea sound to you today?

2. Where are you in the spiral of acceptance? Which of your behaviors and attitudes are similar to the women who were interviewed for the research? Which are dissimilar? Which of these behaviors and attitudes would you like to change? To keep?

3. If you were being interviewed for this kind of study, what kinds of things might you say to the researcher about your process of body-size acceptance? How would you describe your current relationship with your body?

4. How do you feel about where you are in your process of size-acceptance? Are you comfortable where you are? Are there some things you would like to change?

5. Think about your ideal relationship with your body. What would you be thinking about yourself? Feeling about your body? Doing with your life?

6. If you have done any of the activities in the "Practical Ideas" section of this chapter, write about your experiences doing them. For instance, how is it to keep track of your accomplishments? What is it like to use positive self-talk? What negative cultural ideas about being fat have you positively reframed? What has been the world's response to your acting as if? Keep track of the methods and techniques that work for you in your process of building size-esteem.

7

If You're Considering Therapy . . .

After working for six years as a counselor in a private college, I applied for another counseling position at a local community college. The initial interview for this particular job was a bit unsettling. I sat before a panel of six people—counselors, administrators, and one student—who fired questions at me from all directions. Since that was my first (and last) group interview, I left wondering what had happened in that room, chalked it up as good experience, and went on. I didn't think they would offer me the job. But they did.

Later I learned that one person on the hiring committee, a counselor, had mentioned my weight as a shortcoming. My weight? What did my weight have to do with my qualifications for this job? Apparently this counselor believed that my weight was an indicator of emotional instability and told the committee as much. I was shocked. Floored. Astounded. Confused. A counselor had said that? And a humanistic counselor at that?

This incident was the first time I was aware of being affected by the prejudices and stereotypes that members of my own profession have about fat people. Unfortunately it hasn't been the last.

I am in a unique position to talk about the subject of therapy for larger women because I've experienced what it's like to grow up fat and to be a fat client in therapy. I'm also a therapist, and I have been fed the same psychological stereotypes about fat people that every other therapist has been exposed to in our professional training. Being humanistically oriented, being holistic and wellness oriented, even being spiritually oriented does not guarantee the elimination of fat-phobia from the consultation room. What this means for you as a larger woman is that if you decide to go into therapy, your size will probably (but not always) be an issue for your therapist, even if it isn't an issue for you.

Because I am acutely aware of this prejudice in the counseling profession, and because I know that many larger women are in therapy for various reasons, I need to address my concerns here. If you aren't currently considering therapy, you might want to skip this chapter for now. But if you are thinking about therapy, or if you have been in therapy, please read on. This is the larger woman's guide to the professional service of psychotherapy.

In chapter 1 I mentioned that there are psychological theories about fatness, which, although not supported by research, proliferate in the profession. Freud, the founding father of psychoanalytic theory, was known to dislike fat people. He theorized that fat people were stuck in the infantile oral stage of development. Other psychoanalytic theories have us repressing our anger and sexuality. The behaviorists theorize that we've learned to respond to hunger by external cues instead of internal ones. Body-work therapists believe we are armoring ourselves, keeping memories and people away by building a wall of body fat.

Add to this list the newer theories: All fat people have eating disorders (addictions theory, Overeaters Anonymous: "Thinness will not make you well, but wellness will make you thin"); all fat women have been sexually abused (eating disorders, addictions theory, Roseanne Arnold, and Oprah Winfrey); all fat women are symbolically, through their fat, telling the world they are angry and want to be seen as powerful and strong (Susie Orbach, *Fat Is a Feminist Issue*); all fat people are depressed (Janet Greeson, *It's Not What You're Eating, It's What's Eating You*); all fat women are angry at their mothers (Judy Hollis, *Fat and Furious*); and all fat women are so because they don't believe they deserve to be thinner (Marianne Williamson, *A Return to Love* and *A Woman's Worth*, new age theory). By the time you read this there will probably be more.

While it is true that some fat women have eating disorders, some fat women have been sexually abused, some fat women are angry, some fat women are depressed, some fat women have bad relationships with their mothers, and some fat women feel undeserving, it is also true that not-fat women have these issues too. Being thin gives no guarantee that these problems won't exist, nor does being fat give an absolute prediction that they will. Since most of these theorists work from the assumption that being fat is pathological (sick), they believe that these problems automatically come with the territory of being a larger woman.

I am not saying that these theorists are intentionally trying to harm fat women. Quite the contrary. I believe they think they are helping us. But they only have a theory, which by definition is not a proven fact. Theories are made by observations, which are always slanted according to the point of view of the observer. Since most of the people who are making up these theories perceive (and thus believe) that fat is bad and that fat people are psychologically unhealthy, they keep coming up with more theories to justify helping us change (lose weight) to fit their perceptions of who is psychologically healthy (not-fat people). If any of these theorists changed their perception, their truth, to affirm that diversity of size was a fact of being human, and not a psychological state of illness, then their attempts at "helping" us would look quite different. In fact, their helping would probably look a lot like the message of *Nothing to Lose*, which is that size-acceptance leads to better self-care, improved self-esteem, and a better quality of life.

So how can you find your way through the maze of theories and therapists in order to find the best one to assist you in your pursuit of size- and self-acceptance and healthier self-esteem? Some of the steps (to be explained in more detail subsequently) are being familiar with the diversity theory of human size; educating yourself about the process of therapy; getting referrals; interviewing potential therapists; and using the feeling of shame as an indicator of your progress in therapy.

To find the right therapist you have to start with this truth about your size: You are part of the grand plan of the diversity in nature. Remember the woman quoted earlier who noticed how no two trees, blades of grass, or snowflakes are alike? Well, look around. That observation is true for people too. This forms the diversity theory of human size, which is another point of view, another perception, and another truth. Having the diversity theory as your truth completely changes the way you look at the world, and it changes the way you observe yourself and other fat women. It makes room for size- and self-acceptance in the body you already have, because everybody has a different body!

If you see the world through the eyes of the diversity theory, then choosing a psychotherapist can be a lot easier. All you have to do is find one who also ascribes to this theory—or at least a therapist who is willing to learn about this theory and to be open to it as the direction in which your therapy is heading: size-acceptance and increased self-esteem, with its accompanying behavior of healthful eating (no dieting) and movement for pleasure and health (not for weight loss).

How do you find a therapist who fits this description? The best way is through referral from others who have had success with their therapists. Another way is through organizations or publications that promote size- and self-acceptance. Publications such as *Radiance* often carry ads from size-friendly therapists, and organizations such as the National Association to Advance Fat Acceptance (NAAFA) and the Association for the Health Enrichment of Large People (AHELP) give referrals too (see endnotes for more information).

If you can't find a therapist through a referral, your search will have to be based on educating yourself about therapy (a good idea for anyone about to enter therapy). Then you'll be in a better position to choose the right therapist for you. Here are a few basics to help you understand therapy.

First, you must understand that therapy is a relationship, a special relationship that is different from the kind you have with your family or friends. In order to enter into this unique relationship, you must feel you can work with this person and that you can learn to trust her or him.

Second, therapy uses the basic tool of effective communication for the sole purpose of helping you learn to behave in new ways that will work better for you than your old behavior did.

Third, the primary goal of a successful therapeutic relationship is your increased self-awareness and self-acceptance. Therapy is a collaborative process: Your therapist is a teacher who facilitates self-discovery, and you are an active agent in your educational process. You do your part by becoming more self-aware, by recognizing areas for change, and by having a willingness to take some degree of risk in changing your perceptions and behavior.

Because there are many types of educational degrees that qualify someone to be a therapist, you may feel confused about which degree is best. Yet degrees are not always the best predictor of successful therapy; effective (and ineffective) therapists can be found with or without certain degrees and titles.

Choosing whether you want to work with a male or a female therapist is an important consideration when it comes to body-image issues. Each has pluses and minuses. The plus column for a female therapist includes the likelihood that she will feel empathy for you, since every woman in this culture (including her) is affected by body-image and weight issues. However, this can also be a detriment. Female therapists learn the same cultural prejudice against fat people that the rest of us learn. Because of this, a female therapist may have a blind spot: She may not recognize her unconscious issues about her body and her learned prejudices about fat people. This will seriously hamper her ability to see you clearly in therapy.

Male therapists are likely to understand the problem of body image differently than female therapists do. This is a plus, because a male is less personally identified with the problem, which allows him a degree of objectivity. The minus side of working with a male, however, is that because he also grew up in this culture, his ideal of a healthy and attractive female body will probably be the same as the culture's. Having this kind of bias will affect how he sees your weight when working with you.

How will you know which therapist, male or female, will be best for you? As in the case of varying degrees and titles, the gender of the therapist may not be the most important predictor of successful therapy, since effective and ineffective therapists can be found in both.

The bottom line in choosing a therapist, regardless of titles, degrees, or gender, is this: The best therapist for you is one you feel you can learn to trust. If your goals are size- and self-acceptance, your trust will be built on your therapist's personal and professional philosophy about fat people, weight, and size issues. So if you communicate to your (potential) therapist that you have a preference for the diversity theory of size rather than the sickness theory of fat, her response will give you clues as to whether or not you would feel comfortable working with her. (Since most women usually prefer working with a female therapist, I will use *her* and *she* when referring to all therapists, male or female, throughout the rest of this section.)

You can use the following questions as a guideline when you interview a potential therapist. Listen for answers that are right for you. Begin with

1. How would you describe the kind of therapy you do?
2. What kinds of clients do you normally work with?

Everyone, whatever their issues, who is considering a therapist should ask these two basic questions. Answers to these questions will vary depending on the therapist's training and interests. How you feel about her answers will be affected by your own situation and preferences. In question 1, for instance, if you prefer to keep your family out of your therapy, it would be a bad match if the therapist says she focuses on family work and would want to see your significant others as part of your treatment. Another example: You have limited money and would prefer short-term therapy, and the therapist does only long-term psychoanalysis.

The second question addresses the kinds of clients the therapist prefers—women, addicts, couples, people with eating disorders, families, kids, and so on—and will help you gauge the compatibility of your interests. When the answers to questions 1 and 2 satisfy you, move on to these, which deal more specifically with size-acceptance:

3. What are your thoughts about fat people? Or: What are your thoughts about working with larger women?

4. Do you believe that all fat (larger) women have eating disorders? (This is especially important to ask a therapist who specializes in eating disorders.)

5. Do you believe that all fat (larger) women have been sexually abused?

6. How do you feel about dieting? Under what circumstances (if ever) would you recommend or support dieting for your clients? Do you diet?

7. Do you feel that someone is healthier, happier, and more attractive if they lose weight? Why? Why not?

8. As a psychotherapist, how do you feel weight can be related to client problems?

9. What do you know about the problems of fat people that are attributable to their social discrimination?

10. Do you have a size-friendly office? Do you have armless chairs available that are more comfortable for a larger person? Do you subscribe to size-friendly magazines such as *Radiance* for your waiting room?

11. I am a larger woman who believes that I can be healthy and happy regardless of weight. My goal is to become more size- and self-accepting. Do you believe this is a realistic goal for my therapy if I work with you?

Not all of these questions (3–10) may be relevant, necessary, or important to ask during the first therapist contact (usually by phone). But communicating the core idea of the diversity theory and size-esteem (question 11) to a potential therapist is of utmost importance if you are to reach your goals of size- and self-acceptance.

How a therapist answers these questions is obviously very important. You may hear responses to your questions that leave you feeling good about the initial contact. This is a therapist with whom you can seriously consider making a first appointment. You may hear responses that leave you feeling that this therapist is on another planet when it comes to this issue. If this happens, thank her for her time and call someone else.

You may hear responses to your questions that leave you feeling ambivalent—some answers you're comfortable with, and others might create a problem. For example, the therapist may give you a double message: She doesn't promote dieting for her clients, yet she still diets on occasion. If something like this happens, you might want to consider the possibility of educating your therapist about your view of dieting and size acceptance if you were to enter into a therapeutic relationship with her. You can do this by asking her if she would be willing to read some material and possibly consider another point of view. If her answer is no, move on. If her answer is yes, you can proceed with making the first appointment, when you can explore these issues in more detail.

This kind of situation came up with my therapist. I knew about her because of her good reputation; when I met her, I immediately liked her. I was also aware that she (understandably) believed some of the culture's stereotypes about fat people. I told her that I had to feel completely safe with her when it came to my weight and size, and I asked her if she would be willing to read some materials about my point of view. I also asked her if she would listen to *my* experience as a larger woman. She agreed. She also invited me to point out to her any traces of fat-phobia that became evident in our working together. These agreements up front not only strengthened our collaborative working relationship but also gave her another point of view. Because my therapist was open to learning something new from me, I felt safe enough to explore issues other than size and weight with her.

Finally, a word about shame and how it can be used as an indicator of your progress in therapy. Shame is a feeling common to women yet rather complex to understand. I believe two things about shame: First, it is an emotion that comes from the gap we feel between our actual self and our ideal self. Second, shame is an emotion that often emerges when our personal experience deviates from what the culture tells us is OK.

Shame is also about feeling alone, cut off from others, isolated, and being secretive, unable to talk about something. Shame is about believing you are a bad person, which is different from thinking you have done a bad thing (which is guilt). Shame is deeply woven into women's feelings about our bodies since our bodies rarely conform to the culture's definition of acceptable, which makes us "deviant." And since the gap between a woman's actual body and her "ideal" body (which is defined by the culture and internalized by the woman as her own desire) is enormous, most women feel shame on a daily basis. How many times have you heard women (including yourself) say, "I feel fat"? What we really mean by this is "I feel bad." Saying we "feel fat" has become an acceptable way to express our shame, a shorthand way to let everyone know that we have failed in some tangible way, symbolized by our imperfect body.

If shame affects women of all sizes, then shame looms large for larger women. Shame has been dumped on us by a culture that believes that we have gone out of control. We are shamed for our size publicly—by strangers on the street and by families and well-intentioned friends. This happens because women's appearance, including weight, is not a private matter but a topic for public consideration and discussion. Susan Wooley, an eating disorder specialist and a larger woman herself, summed it up when she said, "If shame could cure obesity, there wouldn't be a fat person in the world."

We all know what shame feels like. Remember this feeling, because if you ever feel that way in your relationship with your therapist, you must let her know. Bringing your shame out of secrecy, where it thrives, and into the light of day, where it can be dealt with, is not to be avoided. But its appearance in therapy might also be an indication that it is time to reevaluate your association with your therapist. With body-size and weight issues, the object of therapy is to reduce shame, not to reduce ourselves to sit at shame's feet once more. Therapy should be a safe place for you in the body you already have.

Psychotherapy is a service for which you are paying your hard-earned money. You have a right to ask for what you want out of the relationship, a right to express your opinions and feelings even if they are different from your therapist's, and a right to set your own goals. This is your therapy and your quality of life, not your therapist's. Please don't settle for less.

Therapy can be a wonderful experience. There is nothing like spending time with someone who is paying complete attention to you; being with someone who really listens to what you're saying (and not saying); being with someone who truly cares about your feelings enough to allow you plenty of room to express them openly (even the ones about her); being with someone who has your well-being, personal growth, and quality of life as her top priority; being with someone who will let you leave when *you* are ready, and who will send you off to face the rest of your life trusting yourself, your perceptions, your experiences, and your value as a woman of size and substance, even if the rest of the world sees you differently.

8

A Story to Feed the Soul: The Tale of Abundia

Once upon a time just last week, a clan of people lived close to the sea. They were tall like the luva tree, which grew at the water's edge, with eyes as dark as the sky before a storm and hair the color of the seagulls' wings. Forever, as long as they could remember, they fished the living waters for food. Lately and inexplicably, the only fish they ate, the zuzulu, were becoming scarcer by the day. The people were beginning to worry about the disappearing zuzulu, because they had nothing else to eat. With each passing month they were getting hungrier and hungrier. And most of them were getting thinner and thinner.

Except for the girl-child Abundia. Named after the ancient goddess of abundance, Abundia was as round as the full moon she was born under, with eyes as blue as the water she was born next to and hair the color of dancing fire. So while the rest of the clan got thinner, Abundia remained round. The clanspeople, already wary of this girl who looked different from them, began to eye her even more suspiciously when the zuzulu fish began to vanish. Did Abundia harbor a secret cache of zuzulu, which she ate by herself? Did she fish at night, catching all the zuzulu, while everyone slept? How could she remain so fat when most everyone else was losing weight, becoming reed-thin?

Abundia wondered about this too. She knew she was eating what the rest of the clan was eating—very little these days—so how could she remain plump while they lost weight? Even though she grew taller, her shape didn't change. She was still round and full.

Even as a toddler Abundia knew she looked different from her clan and that her differentness caused them to act cautiously around her. She realized that now most of them mistrusted her. She started to feel ashamed of her body. She felt lonely too since the children teased her about her size and appearance. She felt like an outsider.

Abundia's grandmother, however, was a comfort to her. Holding Abundia close at night, Grandmother would tell Abundia that she was special. You see, Grandmother thought the goddess probably had a plan for Abundia. So she wisely advised Abundia to make room in her heart for the children and people of her clan, since they were not only hungry, they were also scared.

One day, after some children teased Abundia about her appetite and size, she wandered down to the sea, which always gave her a sense of peace. She decided to forget her troubles, put her toes into the water, and play tag with the waves. The waves didn't care if she was fat! They would play with her.

As she chased the waves along the shore, she lost track of time and distance. In fact, she had gone so far that she didn't recognize where she was. But the sea seemed to be inviting her to come in. So she knotted up her hair, took off her clothes, and swam out to a huge rock that jutted out of the water. As she swam, Abundia noticed how easily she was able to float in the water, as if she were being held by the gentle, rocking waves.

When Abundia reached the rock, she untangled her long fiery locks, allowing them to billow free in the breeze, and stared out at the vast blue emptiness. She finally felt at peace.

After some time had passed, Abundia was jolted out of her tranquillity by an eerie sound, like the wind forcing itself through a small crack. Then, right in front of her sea-blue eyes, there emerged a roundish woman, dazzling in silvery white light. This woman reminded Abundia of the brightest, fullest full moon she had ever seen. Abundia noticed that the woman carried a large basket filled with brightly colored objects of all shapes and sizes. These objects were actually fruits and vegetables, but since Abundia had never seen fruits and vegetables before, she didn't know what they were.

The woman spoke to Abundia. "You are my namesake, Abundia, my godchild, and I love you dearly. Lately you have been feeling ashamed of your body because of its appearance, which is different from that of your clanspeople, and you have been mistreated by those who do not understand your destiny. You have been given this plump, round body for a reason, Abundia, which will be revealed to you in time. But first you must discover three things about yourself. You must find your beauty, your voice, and your purpose. To do this you must leave your home and travel to the land beyond the sea. Do not be afraid, for I shall be close by. I shall come to you often in your dreams, and you shall also hear me speak to you as a voice from your heart." Then the beautiful woman dissolved into a mist and was gone.

Abundia, astonished and scared, nevertheless felt strangely lighter and more hopeful than she had felt in a long time. She swam to the shore, dressed, and ran home as fast as her chubby legs could carry her.

When she told Grandmother what had happened, Grandmother smiled and nodded. It had been a long time since the goddess of abundance had appeared to one of her people, and Grandmother knew her people had forgotten about the goddess over the years. She now understood, however, that her grandchild's destiny would be to bring this goddess back into the life of their clan. So Grandmother told Abundia that she would miss her, but that Abundia would have to do what the goddess required of her. While Abundia prepared for her journey by bathing and putting on fresh clothes, her grandmother packed her a basket filled with dried zuzulu fish. Then she sent Abundia on her way with a kiss.

Abundia traveled to the land beyond the sea, which proved to be closer than she had imagined. She saw so many new and different plants and animals in the valleys and woods that she couldn't believe her eyes. She was tempted at first to find the diverse colors, sizes, and shapes disagreeable, but a voice from her heart told her that although no two flowers, trees, or birds were identical, they were all beautiful. Abundia agreed with her heart and enjoyed looking at the loveliness around her.

Suddenly Abundia realized something new: She could look different from the rest of her clan and still be beautiful! The tall yellow flowers that grew in the fields were every bit as lovely as the delicate blue flowers she found in the woods. Once she understood this truth, which came from her heart, she saw it everywhere she traveled. She gradually grew more accepting of her size and body and beauty just as they were.

After a time, Abundia ran out of the dried zuzulu fish her grandmother had packed, and she got very hungry. In fact, she got so hungry that one night she cried herself to sleep. During her sleep that night, Abundia dreamed of the goddess and her basket of colorful and different-shaped objects. The goddess told Abundia that since she had discovered the secret of her own beauty, she was ready to discover the beauty and usefulness of the objects in the basket. "My basket contains food," said the goddess. "In finding this food, which grows everywhere, you will be able to nourish yourself and your people. This is also the way you will find your voice, Abundia."

When Abundia woke from her dream, she looked at the woods around her and began to see them differently. They were not only beautiful in their own way, but they also showed themselves to be a source of food. Remembering the objects in the goddess's basket, Abundia looked around and found big red balls that grew on trees and little blue balls that grew on bushes. She sampled them and found that they tasted delicious. She dug up roots that smelled earthy and tasted hearty. She discovered that stalks and vines had their share of goodies too.

The goddess kept her promise to Abundia and stayed close to her, guiding her while she dreamed. She told Abundia that she was finding fruits and vegetables, with names like apples, blueberries, carrots, potatoes, corn, and grapes. Pretty soon Abundia realized that there was an abundance of food to eat beyond the zuzulu fish. She was excited about her new learning and couldn't wait to go home to share it with her people, to tell them that in the woods and valleys, not far from home, there was plenty to eat.

Abundia packed her basket with her newfound sources of nourishment and went back to the clan to share her good news. When she arrived, however, they weren't at all pleased with her discovery. In fact, they thought she was crazy. Eat a red ball that grows on trees? An orange root from the ground? Whoever heard of such a thing? They were hungry and cranky and accustomed to eating only the zuzulu fish. Nothing Abundia said could persuade them to eat what she had discovered. This is food? Harrumph!

Grandmother did believe Abundia, however, and was proud of what Abundia had learned on her travels. She sensed a different child from the one who had left her a few months before—more sure of herself and happier. Grandmother trusted what Abundia said and cheerfully tasted the fruits and vegetables. They were delicious! Much better than dried, or even fried, zuzulu fish!

So with Grandmother's support and the goddess's wisdom, Abundia began the task of finding her own voice, speaking her truth to the clan. Since her journey, Abundia felt more comfortable in her larger body, so the adults stopped looking at her with mistrust and displeasure. When the children made fun of her size, she ignored them or told them that she knew she was beautiful, and that was all that mattered. And always Abundia kept this learning close to her heart: There is beauty in diversity.

Abundia also made it her job to convince her clan that there was more to eat in the world than zuzulu fish. She and Grandmother went into the woods and fields and collected as much food as they both could carry. The goddess told Abundia that other fish in the sea were good to eat too. So Abundia and Grandmother went fishing at night until they had made a good haul. They then prepared a feast for the whole clan.

Fortunately the clanspeople were hungry enough to show up for dinner. Cautiously they tasted what was prepared, and although it looked and tasted unusual, they ate it all until they were full, satisfied, happy, pleased, and smiling in wonder at Abundia.

It was during this feast that Abundia realized that her lessons from the goddess were complete. Abundia's beauty was marked by her differentness. Her voice spoke her heart's truth. And her life's purpose was to bring her clanspeople back to the goddess of abundance. By honoring this goddess and her gifts, the whole clan learned that there is no scarcity when one honors diversity and looks at the world abundantly.

Appendix 1

A Word About Dieting and Compulsive Eating

Many of you want to learn to accept your body size yet are troubled by your eating behavior. The spiraling process of body-size acceptance (see chapter 6) reminds us that eating behavior goes through its own transitions as we go through the process of accepting our size. If you have been a lifelong dieter, you can use the spiral of acceptance as a guide to how your eating will probably change over time. You can expect that you will most likely go from dieting to bingeing (typical for anyone who diets) to healthful eating (meaning a process of stabilizing your relationship with food) to the point where food and eating are not the focal point of your life.

What follows is a brief summary of some of the major issues involved with eating, dieting, and bingeing, especially for larger women. It is not intended to be comprehensive.

Many books have been written about these topics, and I encourage you to seek out more information, especially the resources mentioned at the end of this appendix. Be wary of anything that claims to be a nondieting approach but promotes a diet in disguise (*Stop the Insanity* by Susan Powter or *Feeding on Dreams* by Epstein and Thompson, for instance). Also beware of anything that maintains that if you stop compulsive eating, you will become "naturally thin" or will always lose weight as a result (*Feeding the Hungry Heart* and *When Food Is Love* by Geneen Roth, for example).

Now let's look at some of the misunderstandings about fat people, food, and eating. First, there is a stereotype that fat people eat more than thin people do. But studies show that fat people, on the average, do not eat more than thin people. Don't you personally know a thin person who consumes thousands of calories a day yet never gains weight? Or the fat person (maybe you) who eats moderately (say two thousand calories a day) and gains weight? (By the way, starvation studies done on human subjects in the 1950s defined semistarvation as fifteen hundred calories a day. This makes me wonder about diets that prescribe a thousand calories or less. Is this a diet or starvation?)

Continual dieting can create havoc when we want to normalize our eating. In the words of a close friend, "I'm either on a diet or off a diet. I'm never just sitting down having dinner!" When we diet, restraining our eating to fewer calories, we deprive our bodies of what they need to function. When we go off a diet, which has deprived us physically and psychologically, we usually binge. Chronic dieters endlessly cycle from deprivation to bingeing to deprivation to binge-ing. In this cycle we never learn how to get back in touch with our own body, our physical hunger, and to eat naturally, with food just being food, which we think about and eat when we are hungry. Can you imagine a life where food and eating are not issues for you? You can begin this process by not dieting.

Compulsive eating is another problem often caused by dieting. Compulsive eating, simply defined, is eating for reasons other than physical body hunger. Compulsive eating can be problematic for women of any size. Unfortunately many doctors, psychotherapists, and nutritionists take one look at a larger woman and assume she is either a compulsive eater or a compulsive overeater and then classify her as having an eating disorder. These may indeed be problems for some large women. However, many large women do not suffer from any eating disorders and have healthy eating habits. Moreover, almost everyone overeats at some point, almost everyone eats from emotional need rather than physical hunger at some point, and almost everyone eats for the sheer pleasure of tasting delicious food at some point. None of these, done occasionally, indicates that you are a compulsive eater, overeater, or have an eating disorder.

Research has also shown that dieting in fact contributes to weight gain with each successive diet for some people. This is known as diet-induced obesity. In other words, you lose fifteen pounds and gain back twenty, lose twenty and gain back thirty-five, and so on. This person winds up fatter after her last diet than she was before the first diet. This is why dieting, which has been offered as the solution to being fat, is the very reason some people get fat!

Finally, dieting and weight loss carry health risks. What are these risks? A partial list includes gallstones, cardiac disorders, fainting, weakness and fatigue, elevated cholesterol, anemia, hypotension, cold intolerance, loss of lean tissue, gastrointestinal problems, hair loss, and even death. We have heard a lot about the health risks of being overweight, but the prescribed solution, dieting, doesn't seem to be much better.

If you would like to find out more about these topics, I recommend the following books, which include a size-acceptance philosophy. They are *Making Peace with Food* by Susan Kano; *Beyond Dieting* by Donna Ciliska; *Overcoming Overeating* and *When Women Stop Hating Their Bodies* by Hirschman and Munter; and *Fed-Up!* by Terry Garrison. *The Health Risks of Weight Loss* by Frances Berg (obtained through the *Healthy Weight Journal*, 701-567-2646) gives a comprehensive look at the research done on dieting (including the starvation study mentioned in this section) up to 1993.

Appendix 2

If You're a Therapist Reading This . . .

People in the helping professions have significantly contributed to the continuing discrimination against fat people. Psychotherapists have made their own unique contributions to this prejudice by trying to provide psychological explanations and treatment for what is clearly a cultural problem. Therapists have been confronted about their biases concerning every other special interest group, including the disabled, gays and lesbians, the elderly, and culturally diverse clients, but they have not yet faced their prejudice about fat people. This appears to be the last socially sanctioned stigma, because unlike being epileptic or gay or old or Hispanic, being fat is still seen as the person's own fault. I believe that therapists have a responsibility to examine their attitudes and stereotypes about fat people, or they will continue to be part of the problem instead of part of the solution.

If you're a therapist and don't believe that bias against fat people is a rampant problem in the profession, I offer you the following quotes taken from a chapter called "The Fat Lady" in the book *Love's Executioner and Other Tales of Psychotherapy* (1989) by the eminent psychiatrist Irvin Yalom.

I have always been repulsed by fat women. I find them disgusting: their absurd sideways waddle, their absence of body contour—breasts, laps, buttocks, shoulders, jaw lines, cheekbones, *everything*, everything I like to see in a woman, obscured in an avalanche of flesh. . . . How dare they impose that body on the rest of us? (P. 88)

Dr. Yalom continues his diatribe against fat people:

Of course I am not alone in my bias. Cultural reinforcement is everywhere. Who ever has a kind word for the fat lady? But my contempt surpasses all cultural norms. . . . When I see a fat lady eat, I move down a couple of rungs on the ladder of human understanding. I want to tear the food away. To push her face into the ice cream. "Stop stuffing yourself! Haven't you had enough, for Chrissakes?" I'd like to wire her jaw shut. (Pp. 88–89)

When I read this (and the rest of the chapter), I was stunned at Yalom's candor and honesty, angered at his blatant prejudice, and saddened that he, a therapist, would feel that way about anyone. It also alerted me to how deeply ingrained these attitudes are and to the fact that a person's education, professional credentials, and respectability do not guarantee the absence of bigotry.

Interestingly enough, the same year *Love's Executioner* was published, another book came out dealing with this topic from a feminist perspective. *Overcoming Fear of Fat* by Laura Brown and Esther Rothblum (eds.) carried this message:

> We have just begun to integrate anti-fat-oppressive perspectives into the practice of psychotherapy. To do so, we must overcome within ourselves and our colleagues long and firmly held prejudices about the value of being thin. We must deal with our own fears of our female bodies, of being ample, taking space, carrying weight. (P. 3)

Yalom, Brown, and Rothblum are respected in their field yet (obviously) do not share the same point of view when working with fat women. Yalom's fat-is-bad perspective is firmly rooted in our culture, while Brown and Rothblum construe the matter differently. They challenge the belief that fat is equivalent to pathology, and their approach affirms that fat oppression, not fat, is the problem. Yalom blames the individual, while Brown and Rothblum criticize the culture.

Most members of my profession would agree with Yalom, and I have therefore committed myself to exposing therapists to another point of view every chance I get—hence the presence of this appendix in *Nothing to Lose*.

If you as a therapist are interested in broadening your professional understanding of this issue, here are some important questions for you to reflect on: Are you willing to see this issue differently, to shift your focus from fat as a sign of pathology to fat as a cultural phobia? Are you willing to look at your own fat-phobia and deal with it on a personal level?

If you are a female therapist, confronting your own fear of fat will more than likely change the way you feel about your own body and the way you take care of it. Will this personal change be welcomed into your life? As a woman and a therapist, I believe that this change is necessary if female therapists are to provide effective and fair treatment for all women who come into our offices with body image issues, but especially for larger women.

If you are a male therapist, are you willing to confront your fat prejudice by becoming aware of how looksism, weightism, and sexism play a role in your involvement with the women in your personal life? Yalom, as a male, reveals that his fat prejudice is partially based on his attraction to thin women and that this is culturally sanctioned. As a therapist, Yalom understands that his preference was also influenced by his personal relationship with the "fat-controlling" women in his family, particularly his mother. Are you willing to do the same kind of soul-searching to understand the roots of your fat-phobia?

If you have given thought to these questions and considerations and are willing to proceed, I offer the following as a brief guide. If you are serious about changing your personal and professional perspective, you have much more reading and self-reflection to do when you close this book.

1. *Become knowledgeable about weight, size, and body-image issues for women from a historical, cultural, and size-diversity point of view.*

Understanding the historical context in which this issue developed is imperative. Look for the research that supports the size-diversity paradigm rather than the fat-is-bad paradigm. Media reports that support a nondieting, size-acceptance point of view can be found almost every week, so watch for them. They are useful as up-to-date reports that you can share with your clients and colleagues.

2. *Engage in an ongoing examination of your attitudes, and reflect on this issue first as it relates to your personal life. If you are a female therapist, you must examine this issue in terms of how it affects your relationship with your own body. Only then can you honestly examine how you can effectively relate to your larger clients.*

Brown and Rothblum believe that therapists need to acknowledge their own fat-oppressive attitudes without shame and then to become engaged in a consciousness-raising experience for more self-awareness. This will ensure that therapists are not fostering a prejudicial climate toward fat, fat people, or themselves.

3. *Be aware of the ethics of working with clients who have food and body-image issues while you are in the process of raising your own consciousness about these same issues.*

Brown and Rothblum believe that it would be unethical for therapists who are in the initial stages of developing their own awareness about food, eating, weight, and body image to work with clients who have these same issues. They suggest that therapists instead spend their time creating a "non-fat-oppressive attitude" in their personal and professional support and consultation groups.

4. *Make the decision to work with larger women as clients once you have established a nondieting size-acceptance viewpoint in your*

own life. You will then be more comfortable using it as an option in treatment.

It is important to know whether a nondieting size-acceptance perspective is one you can work with when you enter into treatment with larger women. You have to consider the ethics of continuing to treat larger women under the old paradigm once you now know that diets don't work and that there isn't one shred of evidence to support the standard psychological theories about fat people. In addition, if you do not have this point of view in your own life, then you will send a double message to your client: "It's OK for you to stop dieting and accept your body, but it's not all right for me." If this is the case, you would probably do better to refer these clients elsewhere.

If you can move in this direction, then you need to develop alternative treatment approaches. You can get some insight into this by examining the various themes in *Nothing to Lose* that come from interviews with women who have learned to accept their body size and by using the spiral of acceptance as a model for this process. You could also use *Nothing to Lose* as bibliotherapy for your individual clients or as a basis in support and therapy groups for larger women (see appendix 3). The other books that I have suggested throughout could also be used for support and guidance in this process.

More important, we need to empower our larger women clients with both the knowledge and the right to confront us if fat-phobic attitudes surface in our therapy sessions with them.

I would like to make this one final point: Not all therapists will be suited to work with these clients, nor will all our clients be ready for the kinds of interventions that this appendix advocates. Pushing a client to accept her body size before she is ready would be ineffective. Having a size-accepting attitude about yourself and your clients, however, will provide an environment where they might begin to assimilate a similar attitude or at least be open to this as an option. As in all counseling and therapeutic situations, the ethical responsibility of the professional is to be fully prepared to deal with his or her own issues while moving clients along with their chosen goals.

If you would like to have more information about this topic, please refer to Brown and Rothblum, editors of *Overcoming Fear of Fat.* I would also like to recommend several other professional articles that examine the role of therapy in the treatment of fat people:

"Confronting the Failure of Behavioral and Dietary Treatments for Obesity" by Garner and Wooley, in *Clinical Psychology Review* 11 (1991): 729–80.

"Ethical Issues in the Treatment of Weight-Dissatisfied Clients" by Connors and Melcher, in *Professional Psychology: Research and Practice* 24, 4 (1993): 404–8.

"Alternatives in Obesity Treatment: Focusing on Health for Fat Women" by Burgard and Lyons, in *Feminist Perspectives on Eating Disorders,* ed. Fallon, Katzman, and Wooley, 1994.

"To Be Recovered and Fat" by Marcia Hutchinson, in *Full Lives: Women Who Have Freed Themselves from Food and Weight Obsession,* ed. Hall, Gurze Books, 1993.

Appendix 3

A Support Group Based on Nothing to Lose

Although most of you reading *Nothing to Lose* are using it as a personal guide to body-size acceptance, some readers may want to form a group to discuss the ideas presented here.* What I present here is only a suggested guide. You can use, change, modify, delete, or rearrange it as you and your group see fit. Trust yourself to know what you need.

*This guide might also be useful to therapists who are interested in starting a therapy group for women who want to become more size- and self-accepting. A therapy group focus, as any therapist knows, will be more feeling-related and unstructured. However (and I cannot emphasize this enough), if you are a therapist doing this work, you must help your clients accumulate the knowledge they need to support a nondieting size-acceptance paradigm. Because the culture is so strongly entrenched in the dieting and thinness-at-any-cost paradigm, dealing exclusively with feelings about body size won't be enough to counter the culture's message. Therefore a psycho-educational approach may be more suited to this work. For a model of this kind of group, see *Beyond Dieting: Psycho-educational Interventions for Chronically Obese Women: A Non-Dieting Approach* by Donna Ciliska (Bruner/Mazel, 1990).

You can gather a group to discuss this without a professional facilitator. Keep in mind, however, that a support group is different from a therapy group. Members of a support group will read primarily on their own and then come together to discuss ideas, share thoughts and feelings, and generally support one another while going through this process. A support group will often be structured with assigned topics and readings to be done between meetings.

The guideline that follows is designed for a closed group (meaning no new members are added after it has begun) with a maximum of eight participants, who meet for approximately two hours each session. Changes can be made to accommodate your group's particular circumstances. As a rule, I encourage group members to read between meetings and to keep a journal about personal responses to the readings and group meetings.

Nothing to Lose *Support Group*

WEEK 1:   Introductions of group members, including why they came and what they expect to get from participating. Everyone takes a turn speaking.

Discuss the format of your group, deciding such things as the readings, discussion length, individual participation in discussions, keeping time, and whether or not to have discussion leaders.

Discuss ground rules for your group, and agree on policies concerning attendance, dropping out of the group, confidentiality, and related matters.

Set up the next group (date, time, place). Assign the "Introduction" and "A Word About Compulsive Eating and Dieting" in *Nothing to Lose* (*NTL*) for discussion at the next meeting.

After the first meeting, begin a personal journal and write about your responses to the group and your related readings.

WEEK 2: Officially begin by warming up to being together. One way is to do a "go-around," meaning each woman has a turn to speak. It's important that everyone say at least one thing at the beginning of the meeting so that everyone will feel included from the start. The go-around for this meeting is to summarize briefly personal responses to the "Introduction" in *NTL*, noting similarities and differences between the author's experiences and your own.

Take turns talking about individual dieting histories and eating issues. Use this time to report on your thoughts and feelings about dieting, your successes and failures.

Discuss the possibilities of not dieting while being in this group. Discuss the personal risks of not weighing yourself for the duration of the group.

If individuals in the group have compulsive eating issues, encourage them to read the books mentioned at the end of that section in *NTL*. Those who do not have eating issues should consider sharing how they have overcome them.

Assign chapter 1 for next week. When reading the chapter at home, highlight those ideas you want to discuss at the next meeting. Journal at home about this meeting and/or the assigned and related readings.

WEEK 3: Officially begin by doing a go-around. One way is to briefly share a thought, feeling, or change of behavior related to food, eating, dieting, or body size since the previous week.

Discuss the various points of interest in the reading, as determined by the group members. It is not important to discuss everything in the chapter. It *is* important to discuss everything that the group members bring up and to have a consensus that closure has been reached on the chapter before moving on.

Decide whether to move on to chapter 2 for the next meeting or to continue discussion with chapter 1.

Journal at home about responses to the meeting and related readings.

WEEK 4:   The format from here on, until the last group, will be similar to week 3.

Officially begin by doing some sort of go-around to warm up to being together. You can use the same one as in week 3, or you can create others.

Discuss what is important from the assigned chapter. Make sure there is consensus that everyone has discussed what's important to them before moving on to the next chapter.

Decide the topic/chapter for the next meeting.

Journal at home about responses to the meeting and related readings.

Last meeting: Same format as the other meetings, except at the end of this meeting the group members decide whether they will continue to meet for another specified period (for example, six or eight more weeks).

At this point people may want to drop out of the group because they feel finished or for other reasons. They should feel free to do so. Make sure that adequate good-byes are said to those who will not be continuing. A way to do this is for everyone to say something positive to those who are leaving—a way they positively affected the group or individuals in the group or a quality they have that members admire. The goal is to have these members leave with a positive experience of the group and of themselves and to allow the remaining group members to feel satisfied with their own good-byes.

Those who decide to continue may want to discuss whether to open the group to new members. Those who continue must remember never to discuss the members who have left. This is an issue of confidentiality.

There are all sorts of variations on this format. You can include other books on topics related to size-acceptance. You may also want to adapt the ideas at the end of each chapter in *NTL* to group exercises. The journal writing ideas can be incorporated for groups whose members like to write. The resources such as films and videos mentioned in *NTL* can be shown and discussed. Perhaps your group could go together to hear a speaker who is coming to your community. If a TV show about this topic airs (it is an endless source of debate on the talk shows), record it and use it for discussion. The possibilities are as varied as the people in the group. Be creative. Have a good time. Open up. Explore new ideas. Share. Listen to others. Avoid giving advice. And always keep in mind that this is a process. It will pay off in the long run.

Notes

Introduction

1. For more information on food intake and size, see Wooley and Wooley, "Should Obesity Be Treated at All?" in *Eating and Its Disorders,* ed. Stunkard and Stellar (Raven Press, 1984). Also see Garner and Wooley, "Confronting the Failure of Behavioral and Dietary Treatments for Obesity," *Clinical Psychology Review II* (1991).

2. For more information on the relationship between size and eating disorders, see Rhodin, Schrank, and Streigel-Moore, "Psychological Features of Obesity," *Med. Clin. N. America,* 73 (1989); *Overcoming Fear of Fat,* ed. Brown and Rothblum; and Marcia Hutchinson, "To Be Recovered and Fat" in *Full Lives,* ed. Lindsey Hall (Gurze Books, 1993).

3. My dissertation, "Nothing to Lose: A Naturalistic Study of Size Acceptance in Fat Women" (1991) can be ordered through University Microfilms International, Publication 91 27666, phone 800-521-0600.

4. For more information on the failure of dieting, see Bennett and Gurin, *The Dieter's Dilemma* (Basic Books, 1982); Dale Atrens, *Don't Diet* (William Morrow, 1988); and Frances Berg, *The Health Risks of Weight Loss* (1993).

5. For more information on the power of myth and stories, see Clarissa Pinkola Estés, *Women Who Run with the Wolves* (Ballantine, 1992).

Chapter 1. Thin Is In—Stout Is Out?

1. For more information on goddess mythology, see Elinor Gadon, *The Once and Future Goddess* (Harper & Row, 1989), and Patricia Monaghan, *Goddesses and Heroines* (Dutton, 1981).

2. The brief history of women's body size and the height-weight charts in this chapter are almost exclusively from Roberta P. Seid, *Never Too Thin: Why Women Are at War with Their Bodies* (Prentice-Hall, 1989). Another good source of information here is Hillel Schwartz, *Never Satisfied: A Cultural History of Diets, Fantasies, and Fat* (Free Press, 1986). For a condensed version of the historical point of view, see "Too 'Close to the Bone': The Historical Context for Women's Obsession with Slenderness" by Roberta P. Seid, in *Feminist Perspectives on Eating Disorders,* ed. Fallon, Katzman, and Wooley (Guilford Press, 1994).

3. For more information on Ancel Keys's study and others that support this point of view, see Paul Ernsberger and Paul Haskew, "Re-Thinking Obesity: An Alternative View of Its Health Implications" in the *Journal of Obesity and Weight Regulation,* 1987.

4. For more information on Dublin's role in changing the definitions of overweight and obesity, again see Seid, *Never Too Thin.*

5. For more information on a recent analysis of the height-weight charts, see the chapter on "Obesity" in *Lifespan: Who Lives Longer and Why* by Thomas J. Moore (Simon & Schuster, 1993).

6. For more information on the Healthy Weight Table, see "Nutrition and Your Health: Dietary Guidelines for Americans," published by the U.S. Department of Agriculture and the U.S. Department of Health and Human Resources, 1990.

7. For more information on Stunkard's definition of obesity as mild, moderate, or severe, see "The Current Status of Treatment for Obesity in Adults" in *Eating and Its Disorders,* ed. Stunkard and Stellar (Raven Press, 1984); and Garner and Wooley, "Confronting the Failure of Behavioral and Dietary Treatments for Obesity" in *Clinical Psychology Review* 11 (1991).

8. For more information on Stunkard's statement about overweight women at risk, see the video *Being Obese,* produced by Grandview Hospital and Medical Center, Health Education Programs, 1985. A copy of the

video can be purchased through Grandview Hospital's Audio Visual Department, 405 Grand Ave., Dayton, OH 45405.

9. For more information regarding Susan Wooley's survey for *Glamour* magazine, see Sternhell, "We'll Always Be Fat But Fat Can Be Fit," *Ms.,* May 1985.

10. For more information on the "Ten Beliefs and Facts" section of this chapter, please see the following:

Belief 1: Dale Atrens, *Don't Diet* (William Morrow, 1988).

Belief 2: Kissileff, Jordan, and Levitz, "Eating Habits of Obese and Normal Weight Humans" in the *International Journal of Obesity* 2 (1978). Wooley and Wooley, "Should Obesity Be Treated at All?" in ed. Stunkard and Stellar, *Eating and Its Disorders.*

Belief 3: Rhodin, Schrank, and Streigel-Moore, "Psychological Features of Obesity," *Med. Clin. N. America,* 73 (1989). Brown and Rothblum, eds., *Overcoming Fear of Fat* (Harrington Park Press, 1989). Hutchinson, "To Be Recovered and Fat" in *Full Lives,* ed. Lindsey Hall (Gurze Books, 1993).

Belief 4: For more information on "pears" and "apples" (body shape) see the National Research Council, *Diet and Health: Implications for Reducing Chronic Disease Risk* (National Academy Press, 1989). For more information on the health benefits of obesity, see Ernsberger and Haskew and Dale Atrens, already cited. The cross-cultural studies on Samoa are from Price's interview with Margaret Mackenzie, "Food Fixations and Body Biases: An Anthropologist Analyzes American Attitudes" in *Radiance,* Summer 1989. The Guam study is "The Influence of Obesity on the Self-Reported Health Status of Chamorros and Other Residents of Guam" by Pinhey, Heathcote, and Rarick in the *Asian American and Pacific Islander Journal of Health* 2, 3 (Summer 1994). Also see Schoenfielder and Weiser, eds., *Shadow on a Tightrope* (Aunt Lute Press, 1983).

Belief 5: See Moore, *Lifespan,* for more information on the high-risk "factors" (rather than "diseases") of obesity, high blood pressure, and high cholesterol. Ernsberger and Haskew for the rest of this section.

Belief 6: Stunkard et al., "An Adoption Study of Human Obesity" in the *New England Journal of Medicine* 314, 4, pp. 193–97, January 1986; and Bouchard et al., "Personality Similarities in Twins Reared Apart and Together" in the *Journal of Personality and Social Psychology* 54, 6, pp. 1031–39, 1988. For more information on the obesity gene (named "ob") see "Researchers Link Obesity in Humans to Flaw in a Gene" in the *New York*

Times, December 1, 1994; "A Gene That Says 'No More,'" in *Newsweek,* December 12, 1994; and "What Really Plumps You Up" in *U.S. News and World Report,* December 12, 1994.

Belief 7: For more information on the set point theory, see Bennett and Gurin, *The Dieter's Dilemma* (Basic Books, 1982). For research supporting the set point theory, see Leibel, Rosenbaum, and Hirsch, "Changes in Energy Expenditure Resulting from Altered Body Weight," *New England Journal of Medicine,* March 9, 1995. For more information on diet-induced obesity, see Seid, *Never Too Thin.* For more on caloric intake of fat people, see Wooley and Wooley, "Obesity and Women I—A Closer Look at the Facts" in *Women's Studies International Quarterly* 2, pp. 69–79, 1979. For a concise, up-to-date look at dieting, see Frances Berg, *The Health Risks of Weight Loss* (1993).

Belief 8: For more information on the FTC investigation of the diet industry, call NAAFA for their newsletters, 916-558-6880. For more information on the use of medication to control weight and fatness, see "Winning the Weight War" produced by the TV news magazine *Forty-eight Hours.* This can be ordered by writing to *Forty-eight Hours* Transcripts, Box 7, Livingston, NJ 07039 (800-777-TEXT). For more information on obesity researchers who own diet companies, see the chapter "Obesity" in Moore, *Lifespan.* For more information on low-fat dieting, see Fraser, "How Low Can We Go?" *Vogue,* January 1994 and Shapiro, "A Food Lover's Guide to Fat," *Newsweek,* December 5, 1994.

Belief 9: Lyons and Burgard, *Great Shape: The First Fitness Guide for Large Women* (Bull Publishing, 1989). Rubin, "Fat and Fit?" in *U.S. News and World Report,* May 16, 1994.

Belief 10: Wooley and Wooley, "Should Obesity Be Treated at All?" in *Eating and Its Disorders,* ed. Stunkard and Stellar. Also see Freedman, *Bodylove* (Harper & Row, 1989); and Burgard and Lyons, "Alternatives in Obesity Treatment: Focusing on Health for Fat Women" in *Feminist Perspectives on Eating Disorders,* ed. Fallon, Katzman, and Wooley.

11. For more information about the 1992 National Institutes of Health report, see "Methods for Voluntary Weight Loss and Control" in the *Annals of Internal Medicine* 116, 11 (1992).

12. For more information on young women who emulate very thin models (the waif look), see the *Healthy Weight Journal,* Summer 1994, published by Frances Berg.

13. For more information regarding the saturated fat and longer life study mentioned in this chapter, see the August 1994 *American Medical Association's Archives of Internal Medicine,* study done by Dr. Steven Grover.

14. For more information on the fitness study showing that slower walkers burn more fat, call the Cooper Institute of Aerobics Research, 800-635-7050, ext. 852. The study was released in 1994.

15. For more information about becoming a healthy larger woman, see the following:

About healthful eating: *Beyond Dieting* by Ciliska (Bruner/Mazel, 1990); *Overcoming Overeating* by Hirschman and Munter (Fawcett Columbine, 1988); *Making Peace with Food* by Kano (Harper & Row, 1989); *Fed-Up!* by Garrison (Carroll & Graf, 1993); "Bodytrust: Undieting Your Way to Health and Happiness," video produced by Dayle Hayes, R.D., 406-656-9417; and the American Dietetic Association, 312-899-0040.

About the relationship between self-esteem and dieting: the dissertation study "Correlates of Self-Esteem, Perceived Control, Body Size Acceptance and Intention to Lose Weight in Women over Two Hundred Pounds" (1991) by Debora Burgard. This can be ordered through University Microfilms, Publication 91 15186, phone 800-521-0600.

About body movement: Lyons and Burgard, *Great Shape;* and Rubin, "Fat and Fit?"

About "getting on with your life": read the rest of *Nothing to Lose!*

Chapter 2. Big Fat Lies

1. For more information on the National Association to Advance Fat Acceptance (NAAFA), call 916-558-6880.

2. For more information on why diets don't work, see Bennett and Gurin, *The Dieter's Dilemma* (Basic Books, 1982); Atrens, *Don't Diet* (William Morrow, 1988); and Garrison, *Fed-Up!* (Carroll & Graf, 1993). Also see Leibel, Rosenbaum, and Hirsch, "Changes in Energy Expenditure Resulting from Altered Body Weight," *New England Journal of Medicine,* March 9, 1995.

3. For more information on therapists' attitudes about larger women, see Yalom, "The Fat Lady" in *Love's Executioner and Other Tales of Psychotherapy* (Basic Books, 1989); and Brown and Rothblum, eds., *Overcoming Fear of Fat* (Harrington Park Press, 1989).

Chapter 3. From the Inside Out: Self-Concept

1. For more information about self-concept and weight-related issues for women, see Susan and Wayne Wooley, "Eating Disorders: Obesity and Anorexia" in *Women and Psychotherapy*, ed. Brodsky and Hare-Mustin (Guilford Press, 1980).

2. For other articles related to self-concept and self-esteem issues for larger women, see the Wooleys again in the following: "Obesity and Women I—A Closer Look at the Facts," and "Obesity and Women II—A Neglected Feminist Topic" in *Women's Studies International Quarterly* 2 (1979). Also, "Should Obesity Be Treated at All?" in *Eating and Its Disorders*, ed. Stunkard and Stellar (Raven Press, 1984).

3. For more information on the benefits of living in the present moment, see *Be Here Now* by Ram Dass (Crown Publishing, 1971), and *On Becoming a Person* by Carl Rogers (Houghton Mifflin, 1961).

Chapter 4. From the Outside In: Body Image

1. For more information on the *Psychology Today* survey, see Cash and Pruzinsky, eds., *Body Images: Development, Deviance and Change* (Guilford Press, 1990).

2. For more information on how cellulite became a common word in women's vocabulary, see Seid, *Never Too Thin: Why Women Are at War with Their Bodies* (Prentice-Hall, 1989), chap. 10.

3. For more information on the cult of low-fat dieting, see Fraser, "How Low Can You Go?" in *Vogue*, January 1994 and Shapiro, "A Food Lover's Guide to Fat" in *Newsweek*, December 5, 1994.

4. For more information on depression and body image, see Noles, Cash, and Winstead, "Body Image, Physical Attractiveness, and Depression" in the *Journal of Consulting and Clinical Psychology* 53, pp. 88–94, 1985.

Chapter 5. Spirit in Action: Involvement in Something Larger Than Ourself

1. For more information on spirit and soul, see Thomas Moore's books, *Care of the Soul* and *Soul Mates*, both published by HarperCollins, 1992 and 1994, respectively.

2. For a further explanation of what being a "professional fat person" means, see Pat Lyons, "What's Up? What's Wrong? What's New?" in *Radiance*, Winter 1991.

3. For more information on humanistic psychology, contact the Association for Humanistic Psychology (AHP), 1772 Vallejo St., San Francisco, CA 94123 (415-346-7929).

4. For more information on how isolation can lead to stress and other unhealthy things, see Taylor, "Healing the Heart" in *New Age Journal*, July/August 1990. Also see Pat Lyons, "Fitness, Feminism, and the Health of Fat Women" in *Overcoming Fear of Fat*, ed. Brown and Rothblum (Harrington Park Press, 1989).

5. For more on the role of support in the lives of size-accepting women, see Marcia Hutchinson, *Transforming Body Image* (Crossing Press, 1985).

Chapter 6. *The Spiral of Acceptance*

1. The TV talk show to which I am referring is the Jerry Springer Show. This particular show was aired on January 4, 1993. The situation being debated between the physician and me was an action being considered by the State of New York. The state was trying to remove two fat girls, ages five and eight, from their home because of their weight (they weighed about 160 and 200 pounds, respectively), charging the parents with neglect. There was no other abuse being reported—no physical, sexual, or emotional abuse. The state felt that the parents were endangering the children's health by allowing them to get fat. The family fought the state and was able to keep the children home, but at great expense to them. A copy of this show can be ordered on videotape by calling 800-FOR VIDEO.

2. My dissertation, "Nothing to Lose: A Naturalistic Study of Size Acceptance in Fat Women" (1991) can be ordered through University Microfilms International, Publication 91 27666 (phone 800-521-0600).

3. For more information on positive self-talk, see books by Aaron Beck, Ph.D., such as *Cognitive Therapy and the Emotional Disorders* (International Universities Press, 1976). Dr. Beck is an originator of using cognitive (thinking) techniques in controlling emotions. Also see *Feeling Good* by David Burns (William Morrow, 1980), and *Bodylove* by Rita Freedman (Harper & Row, 1989).

4. For more information on the technique of reframing as it relates to body image, see Freedman, *Bodylove.*

5. For more information on acting as if, see Roberto Assagioli's books, *Psychosynthesis* and *Act of Will* (Penguin, 1973).

6. For more information about the personal lives of larger women who can act as role models see Carole Shaw, *Come Out, Come Out, Wherever You Are* (American R. R. Publishing, 1982); Nancy Roberts, *Breaking All the Rules* (Penguin, 1985); Clarissa Pinkola Estés, "Joyous Body: Wild Flesh" in *Women Who Run with the Wolves* (Ballantine, 1992); and Carol Wiley, *Journeys to Self-Acceptance: Fat Women Speak* (Crossing Press, 1994).

Chapter 7. If You're Considering Therapy . . .

1. For more information about Freud's view of fat people, see *Glory Reflected: Sigmund Freud, Man and Father* by his son, Martin Freud (Vanguard Press, 1958).

2. For more information on other psychological theories of fatness, see Joel Gurin, "Leaner, Not Lighter" in *Psychology Today,* June 1989.

3. For more information on Overeaters Anonymous, see *Compulsive Overeater* by Bill B. (available through OA's group meetings, 1981). For a critique of Overeaters Anonymous, see Katherine Van Wormer, "Hi, I'm . . . a Compulsive Overeater" in *Feminist Perspectives on Eating Disorders,* ed. Fallon, Katzman, and Wooley (Guilford Press, 1994).

4. For more information about sexual abuse and weight, just read any 1993–94 women's magazine about Roseanne Arnold or Oprah Winfrey (or listen to Oprah's shows about her weight, such as her "Conversations" with larger women and the Geneen Roth shows aired in November 1992 and the discrimination against fat people show aired in 1994). Both Roseanne and Oprah talk about the connection between their own sexual abuse and their eating, hence their weight issues. The problem with this kind of publicity is that they (and everyone else) believe sexual abuse is an issue for most or all fat women.

For a critique of the opinion that sexual abuse and fatness are related, see Nancy Barron, "The Overeating Myth" in *Big Beautiful Woman,* December 1992.

A final note about Oprah: She is also consistent in expressing her view that all overweight people have emotional problems that, unfortunately, show on our bodies. I take no issue with Oprah if this is true for her when she is heavier. However, I do take issue with her when she insists that this is true for all fat people. It isn't.

5. For more information about the symbolic interpretation of women and their fatness, see Susie Orbach, *Fat Is a Feminist Issue* (Berkeley Books, 1978). For a critique of this theory by someone who went through group therapy with the women's psychotherapy center where Orbach worked, see Nancy Roberts, *Breaking All the Rules* (Penguin, 1985). For another critique see Seid, *Never Too Thin* (Prentice-Hall, 1989).

6. For more information about Janet Greeson's program for in-patient treatment of fat women based on their clinical depression, see the March 1994 "Winning the Weight War" on the TV news magazine *Forty-eight Hours*. It can be ordered by writing to *Forty-eight Hours* Transcripts, Box 7, Livingston, NJ 07039 (800-777-TEXT).

7. For more information on fat women and their anger at their mothers, see Judy Hollis, *Fat and Furious* (Ballantine, 1993).

8. For more information on the new age theory of weight control, see Marianne Williamson, *A Return to Love* (for insight into her own weight struggles; HarperCollins, 1992), and *A Woman's Worth* (for her opinions on fat women, pp. 25–28; Random House, 1993).

9. For more information on a healthy psychological look at women's weight and bodies, see Clarissa Pinkola Estés, "Joyous Body: Wild Flesh" in *Women Who Run with the Wolves* (Ballantine, 1992).

10. For more information about our perceptions of the world formed through the social construction of it, see Paul Watzlawik, *The Invented Reality: How Do We Know What We Believe We Know?* (W. W. Norton, 1984).

11. For more information on the diversity theory of human size, see Vivian Mayer, "The Fat Illusion" in *Shadow on a Tightrope,* ed. Schoenfielder and Weiser (Aunt Lute Press, 1983).

12. For more information about subscribing to *Radiance,* call 510-482-0680. For more information about NAAFA's referral services, call 916-558-6880. NAAFA also has some printed material on therapy (pamphlet on eating disorders and NAAFA newsletter June/July 1994). For more information on AHELP, write P.O. Drawer C, Radford, VA 24143.

13. For more information regarding shame, see Judith Rodin, "The Shame Trap" in *Body Traps* (William Morrow, 1992).

14. Susan Wooley's widely used quote on shame is taken from Carol Sternhell, "We'll Always Be Fat But Fat Can Be Fit" in *Ms.*, May 1985.

15. For more complete information on choosing a therapist and the process of therapy, see Karen Johnson, "Using Professional Assistance" in *Trusting Ourselves: The Complete Guide to Emotional Well-Being for Women* (Atlantic Monthly Press, 1991).

Recommended Reading

Books

History of Women's Body Image

Beller, Anne Scott. *Fat and Thin: A Natural History of Obesity.* McGraw-Hill Ryerson, 1977.

Gadon, Elinor. *The Once and Future Goddess.* Harper & Row, 1989.

Monaghan, Patricia. *Goddesses and Heroines.* Dutton, 1981.

Schwartz, Hillel. *Never Satisfied: A Cultural History of Diets, Fantasies and Fat.* The Free Press, 1986.

Seid, Roberta Pollack. *Never Too Thin: Why Women Are at War with Their Bodies.* Prentice-Hall, 1989.

Nondieting Approaches

Atrens, Dale. *Don't Diet.* William Morrow, 1988.

Bennett, William, and Joel Gurin. *The Dieter's Dilemma.* Basic Books, 1982.

Berg, Frances. *The Health Risks of Weight Loss.* Published through the *Healthy Weight Journal,* 1993.

Ciliska, Donna. *Beyond Dieting.* Bruner/Mazel, 1990.

Hirschman, Jane, and Carol Munter. *Overcoming Overeating.* Fawcett Columbine, 1988.

Hirschman, Jane, and Carol Munter. *When Women Stop Hating Their Bodies.* Ballantine, 1995.

Kano, Susan. *Making Peace with Food.* Harper & Row, 1989.

Eating Disorders

Brown, Catrina, and Karen Jasper, eds. *Consuming Passions: Feminist Approaches to Weight Pre-Occupations and Eating Disorders.* Second Story Press, 1993.

Chernin, Kim. *The Hungry Self: Women, Eating, and Identity.* Harper & Row, 1985.

Chernin, Kim. *The Obsession: Reflections on the Tyranny of Slenderness.* Harper & Row, 1981.

Fallon, Patricia, Melanie Katzman, and Susan Wooley, eds. *Feminist Perspectives on Eating Disorders.* Guilford Press, 1994.

Hall, Lindsey, ed. *Full Lives: Women Who Have Freed Themselves From Food and Weight Obsession.* Gurze Books, 1993.

O'Garden, Irene. *Fat Girl: One Woman's Way Out.* HarperSanFrancisco, 1993.

Health and Fitness

Boston Women's Health Collective. *The New Our Bodies Our Selves.* Simon & Schuster, 1992.

Ernsberger, Paul, and Paul Haskew. "Re-Thinking Obesity: An Alternative View of Its Health Implications." *Journal of Obesity and Weight Regulation,* 1987.

Lyons, Pat, and Debora Burgard. *Great Shape: The First Fitness Guide for Large Women.* Bull Publishing, 1988.

Moore, Thomas J. *Lifespan: Who Lives Longer and Why.* Simon & Schuster, 1993.

Northrup, Christine. *Women's Bodies, Women's Wisdom: Creating Physical and Emotional Health and Healing.* Bantam, 1994.

Self-Concept and Self-Esteem

Brandan, Nathaniel. *How to Raise Your Self-Esteem.* Bantam Books, 1987.

Fanning, Patrick, and Matthew McKay. *Self-Esteem.* Gurze Books, 1990.

Sanford, Linda, and Mary Ellen Donovan. *Women and Self-Esteem: Understanding and Improving the Way We Think and Feel About Ourselves.* Anchor/Doubleday, 1984.

Steinem, Gloria. *Revolution from Within: A Book of Self-Esteem.* Little Brown, 1992.

Wolf, Naomi. *The Beauty Myth: How Images of Beauty Are Used Against Women.* William Morrow, 1991.

Body Image

Cash, Thomas, and Thomas Pruzinsky, eds. *Body Images: Development, Deviance and Change.* Guilford Press, 1990.

Freedman, Rita. *Bodylove.* Harper & Row, 1989.

Hutchinson, Marcia. *Transforming Body Image: Learning to Love the Body You Have.* Crossing Press, 1985.

Newman, Leslea. *SomeBody to Love.* Third Side Press, 1991.

Rodin, Judith. *Body Traps.* Quill William Morrow, 1992.

Size Acceptance

Bovey, Shelley. *The Forbidden Body: Why Being Fat Is Not A Sin.* Harper Pandora, 1994.

Edison, Laurie, and Debbie Notkin. *Women En Large.* Books in Focus, 1994.

Garrison, Terry. *Fed-Up! A Woman's Guide to Freedom from the Diet/Weight Prison.* Carroll & Graf, 1993.

Higgs, Liz Curtis. *One Size Fits All and Other Fables.* Thomas Nelson, 1993.

Johnson, Carol. *Self-Esteem Comes In All Sizes: How to Be Happy and Healthy at Your Natural Weight.* Doubleday, 1995.

Mayer, Ken. *Real Women Don't Diet! One Man's Praise of Large Women and His Outrage at the Society That Rejects Them.* Bartleby Press, 1993.

NAAFA. *The NAAFA Workbook: A Complete Study Guide.* NAAFA, 1987.

Naidus, Beverly. *One Size Does Not Fit All.* Aigis Publications, 1994.

Pinkwater, Daniel. *The Afterlife Diet.* Random House, 1995.

Roberts, Nancy. *Breaking All the Rules: Feeling Good and Looking Great No Matter What Your Size.* Penguin Books, 1985.

Rose, Laura. *Life Isn't Weighed on the Bathroom Scales.* WRS Publishing, 1993.

Schoenfielder, Lisa, and Barb Weiser, eds. *Shadow on a Tightrope: Writings by Women on Fat Liberation.* Aunt Lute Press, 1983.

Schroeder, Charles. *Fat Is Not a Four Letter Word*. ChronMed, 1992.

Shaw, Carol. *Come Out, Come Out, Wherever You Are!* American R. R. Publishing, 1982.

Wiley, Carol. *Journeys to Self-Acceptance: Fat Women Speak*. Crossing Press, 1994.

Spirit and Spirituality

Bolen, Jean Shinoda. *Crossing to Avalon*. HarperSanFrancisco, 1994.

Bolen, Jean Shinoda. *The Goddess in Every Woman*. Harper & Row, 1984.

Brown, Sharon, Pat Paulsen, and Jo Ann Wolf. *Living on Purpose*. Simon & Schuster, 1989.

Estés, Clarissa Pinkola. *Women Who Run with the Wolves: Myths and Stories of the Wild Woman Archetype*. Ballantine, 1992.

Monaghan, Patricia. *Seasons of the Witch*. Delphi Press, 1992.

Moore, Thomas. *Care of the Soul*. HarperCollins, 1992.

Psychology and Therapy

Alberti, R. E. *Your Perfect Right: A Guide to Assertive Living*. Impact Publishers Inc., 1989.

Ferrucci, Piero. *What We May Be: Techniques for Psychological and Spiritual Growth Through Psychosynthesis*. Jeremy Tarcher, 1982.

Johnson, Karen. *Trusting Ourselves: The Complete Guide to Emotional Well-Being for Women*. Atlantic Monthly Press, 1991.

Louden, Jennifer. *The Woman's Comfort Book: A Self-Nurturing Guide for Restoring Balance in Your Life*. HarperSanFrancisco, 1992.

Noble, Kathleen. *The Sound of a Silver Horn*. Fawcett Columbine, 1994.

Rogers, Carl. *On Becoming a Person*. Houghton Mifflin, 1961.

Taylor, Shelley. *Positive Illusions: Creative Self-Deceptions and the Healthy Mind*. Basic Books, 1989.

For Therapists

Brown, Laura, and Esther Rothblum, eds. *Overcoming Fear of Fat*. Harrington Park Press, 1989.

Magazines

Big Beautiful Woman (BBW)
213-651-0469, and 800-707-5592 for subscribers

EXTRA! Woman
P.O. Box 57194
Sherman Oaks, CA 91413
818-997-8404

Fat! So?
P.O. Box 423464
San Francisco, CA 94142-3464

Radiance, the Magazine for Large Women
P.O. Box 30246
Oakland, CA 94604
510-482-0680 (fax and phone)

Newsletters and Journals

Food for Thought
c/o Largesse
Resource Network for Size Esteem
P.O. Box 9404
New Haven, CT 06534-0404
203-787-1624 (fax and phone)

Healthy Weight Journal
Healthy Living Institute
402 S. 14th St.
Hettinger, ND 58639
701-567-2646

On a Positive Note
P.O. Box 17223
Glendale, WI 53217

Overcoming Overeating Newsletter
Jade Publishing
935 W. Chestnut, Suite 420
Chicago, IL 60622

Organizations

Abundia
Programs for the Promotion of Body-Size Acceptance and Self-Esteem
P.O. Box 252
Downers Grove, IL 60515
708-897-9796

Ample Opportunity
P.O. Box 40621
Portland, OR 97240-0621
503-245-1524
(also publishes a newsletter)

Association for the Health Enrichment of Large People (AHELP)
P.O. Drawer C
Radford, VA 24143

Body Image Task Force
P.O. Box 934
Santa Cruz, CA 95061
408-426-1821

Bodytrust
2110 Overland Ave.
Suite 120
Billings, MT 59102
1-800-321-9499

Chicago Center for Overcoming Overeating
P.O. Box 48
Deerfield, IL 60015
708-853-1200

Council on Size and Weight Discrimination
P.O. Box 305
Mt. Marion, NY 12456
914-679-1209

Diet/Weight Liberation
Anabel Taylor Hall
Cornell University
Ithaca, NY 14853
607-257-0563

Largely Positive
P.O. Box 17223
Glendale, WI 53217

Largesse
Resource Network for Size Esteem
P.O. Box 9404
New Haven, CT 06534-0404
203-787-1624 (fax and phone)

National Association to Advance Fat Acceptance (NAAFA)
P.O. Box 188620
Sacramento, CA 95818
916-558-6880
916-558-6881 (fax)
(also publishes a newsletter)

National Center for Overcoming Overeating
315 W. 86th St., 17-B
New York, NY 10024
212-875-0442
212-874-6596 (fax)

No Diet Day Coalition
P.O. Box 305
Mount Marion, NY 12456
914-679-1209 (fax and phone)

Acknowledgments

When a book is published, the readers see only the finished product. Yet this kind of work is almost never done by the writer alone, without the help, support, and encouragement of many people along the way. Because this book reflects a personal process that I have been going through my entire life, a multitude of people have contributed to its body, heart, and soul. This is my "thank you" to some of the major contributors to *Nothing to Lose*.

To the women of Abundia, the true midwives of this creation: Sally Strosahl, Jeanette Zweifel, Barbara Spaulding, and Sue Ross.

To Patricia Monaghan, a woman abundant in body, mind, and creative soul, who tirelessly gave me the encouragement, support, information, resources, and contacts I needed to see this move from an idea to a published work.

To Helane Hulburt, my angel-agent.

To Caroline Pincus, my editor, who was waiting for this book to find its way to her. Thank you for recognizing it when it arrived! And thank you for enthusiastically supporting it (and me) throughout the publication process.

To Marilyn Marchetti, who helped me find my voice.

To Jeannie Kokes for giving me room to express my multifaceted self in her presence of total acceptance and love.

To Jerry Perlmutter for getting me through the hard part.

To my academic mentors who supported me and the original research project: Robert Nejedlo, Laura Smart, Paul Ilsley, and Mary Farnum.

To the women who have shared their stories with me, especially the women I interviewed for my study, and the women who have taken my classes and workshops over the years. Thank you for trusting me enough to share your stories of pain and triumph.

To my soul sister, Barbara Robinette, and to my spiritual sisters, Carol Petok, Vicki Koutavas, and Christine Walsh.

To those who have loved me over the years regardless of the shape and size of my body or the condition of my psyche: Art Snedekar, Lois Neville, Lorin Katz, David Rigg, Les Borzy, Nancy Perkins, Bob Pearman, Nancy Lenz, M. J. Hartwell, Jim Frank, Jenna Eisenberg, Sarah Delcourt, Clare Tropp, Kathy Kornbloom, Vicki Knauerhase, Ginger Barson, Carole Damien, Abby Davis, Moya Jones, Bob Berger, Chet Witek, Karen Heifitz, Mike Saba, Mark Scheerer, Marcantonio Squatrito, Mary Gayle Floden, Mary Holdway, Nancy and

Paul Svoboda, Donna Ramberg, Joanne Hill, Tammy De Boer, Jonna Wing, and Norman Chambers.

To those who believed that this book would be born long before I did: Jo Ann Wolf, Susan Koppelman, Joyce Fletcher, Betty Elliott, Jeff Edwards, Debi Harding, Ken Harris, and Lois Bartholomew.

To my professional circle of mentors, colleagues, and friends who are committed to the idea that everyone, especially larger people, have worth: Marcia Hutchinson, Donna Ciliska, Pat Lyons, Jane Benson, Carol Johnson, Alice Ansfield, Rick Zakowich, and Joe McVoy.

To "No Limits for Women Artists," especially Deb Trent.

To Rick Starke of Harper Collins and Joe Durepos of Anderson's Bookstores, who were early and continuing supporters of this work.

To my family: especially my grandmother, Nan, my mother and father, William and Dolores Erdman, and my brothers, Patrick, Michael, Christopher, and Bill Erdman. Thank you for wholeheartedly believing that I could accomplish anything I set my sights on and for expressing that belief to me often.

Finally, to my husband, Terry Jones, whose unconditional love has provided a solid ground for me to walk on and a safety net for me to fall into. Thank you for always loving me just the way I am.